Kanthavel Radhakrishnan
Dhaya Ramakrishnan

LEVERAGING ARTIFICIAL INTELLIGENCE AND MACHINE LEARNING

Kanthavel Radhakrishnan
Dhaya Ramakrishnan

LEVERAGING ARTIFICIAL INTELLIGENCE AND MACHINE LEARNING

PREDICTIVE THREAT HUNTING IN CYBERSECURITY

LAP LAMBERT Academic Publishing

Imprint
Any brand names and product names mentioned in this book are subject to trademark, brand or patent protection and are trademarks or registered trademarks of their respective holders. The use of brand names, product names, common names, trade names, product descriptions etc. even without a particular marking in this work is in no way to be construed to mean that such names may be regarded as unrestricted in respect of trademark and brand protection legislation and could thus be used by anyone.

Cover image: www.ingimage.com

Publisher:
LAP LAMBERT Academic Publishing
is a trademark of
Dodo Books Indian Ocean Ltd. and OmniScriptum S.R.L publishing group

120 High Road, East Finchley, London, N2 9ED, United Kingdom
Str. Armeneasca 28/1, office 1, Chisinau MD-2012, Republic of Moldova, Europe
Managing Directors: Ieva Konstantinova, Victoria Ursu
info@omniscriptum.com

Printed at: see last page
ISBN: 978-620-8-44473-0

LEVERAGING ARTIFICIAL INTELLIGENCE AND MACHINE LEARNING FOR PREDICTIVE THREAT HUNTING IN CYBERSECURITY

Kanthavel R,
School of Electrical and Communications Engineering,
PNG University of Technology, Lae, Papua New Guinea.
kanthavel2005@gmail.com

Dhaya R
School of Electrical and Communications Engineering,
PNG University of Technology, Lae, Papua New Guinea.
dhayavel2005@gmail.com

Abstract:

As cybersecurity threats continue to evolve in sophistication, velocity, and impact, the conventional reactive security approaches cannot keep up with them. In these cases, cyber attackers have employed more sophisticated strategies such as polymorphic malware, fileless attacks, and living-off-the-land techniques that do not depend on traditional detection methods. Anticipating this, predictive risk looking (more notably using artificial intelligence (AI) and machine learning) has emerged as a key technology in today's cybersecurity strategies. Predictive risk finding allows security teams to proactively detect hidden risks, spot anomalies, and anticipate adversary behaviours before it results in a breach or device compromise. AI/ML approaches leverage behavioural analytics, large-scale telemetry data, and real-time learning to uncover overlooked patterns often missed by human analysts or rule-based architectures. In this article, we provide an exclusive overview of today's cutting-edge AI and ML applications in predictive risk looking. We focus on core technologies, device architectures, algorithmic models, and industry specific implementations, while also discussing challenges that include model interpretability, information bias, and counterattacks. It also provides future research roadmaps including the integration of Explainable AI, federated learning frameworks, and Zero Trust architectures.

Index Terms: Cybersecurity, Threat Hunting, Artificial Intelligence, Machine Learning, Predictive Analytics, Intrusion Detection, Anomaly Detection, Network Security, Federated Learning, Explainable AI

1. Introduction

The escalating digital transformation across many sectors has paradoxically increased the difficulty levels in cybersecurity. Today, enterprises control extensive interconnected networks, Internet of Things (IoT) ecosystems, and cloud infrastructures, with each component forming an extension to the attack surface. Traditional defense mechanisms are becoming increasingly ineffective against hyper-evolving threats like Advanced Persistent Threats (APTs), zero-day exploits, and fileless malware [1]. To aggravate the situation are remote working environments, bring-your-own-device policies, and hybrid cloud adoption, which have rendered security perimeters even more fluid. All of these erstwhile solutions warrant a shift to more proactive defense strategies, employing automated algorithms, rather than static rule sets and manual digital investigation. Hence predictive threat hunting stands out as a linchpin of modern-day cybersecurity strategy.

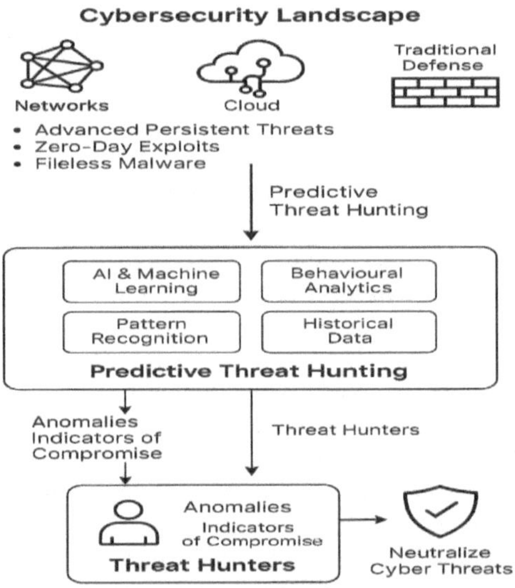

Figure 1: Cybersecurity Landscape

Consequently, rather than simply reacting, the whole notion behind predictive threat hunting is to make use of AI and ML technology to actively seek out cyber threats and obstruct them before they can do any damage. In contrast to signature-oriented approaches, it entails behavioural analytics, pattern recognition, and historical data mining. These tools will enable threat hunters to spot anomalous behaviour and obscure indicators of compromise (IoCs) that may signify an ongoing or future attack by performing data mining. Such a data-driven method contrasts sharply with the traditional defensive model and calls for newly cultivated competencies at Security Operations Centres (SOCs). The AI-ML-yoked processes can automate mundane tasks, reduce false positives, and strive to learn through the evolving threat landscape. These technologies become instrumental in understanding the adversaries' complicated Tactics, Techniques, and Procedures (TTPs), thereby providing the necessary intelligence to the defenders for an effective and proactive response. As illustrated in figure 1 as Cybersecurity Landscape.

This review presents an extended analysis of theories and practices regarding AI and ML in predictive threat hunting from research and practice perspectives. Also highlighted is the evolution of threat hunting along with fundamental architectures and machine learning models, industry-specific applications, benefits, and present limitations. Future research opportunities are briefly sketched out since it can provide a sometimes-penetrating snapshot of how the future might hold by AI and ML in cybersecurity. Predictive threat hunting employs AI and ML techniques and algorithms to uncover and neutralize the cyber threat before inflicting any harm. It differs from the signature-based method since it relies on behavioural analysis, pattern recognition, and historical data mining. This review presents an extended examination of AI/ML-driven predictive threat hunting, from theoretical underpinnings into applied methodologies.

2. Literature Review

As such, cyberattacks are growing in sophistication and frequency, which has compelled businesses to transition from traditional reactive security practices to active predictive ones. While predictive threat hunting based on Artificial Intelligence (AI) and Machine Learning (ML) is a popular, emerging way of identifying and countering more sophisticated cyber threats before they can be damaging .Early studies have highlighted the limitations of traditional signature-based detection methods that fail to detect file-less malware, zero-day exploits (Siddiqui et al, 2018) and living-off-the-land attacks which exploit legitimate processes (Ucci et al., 2019). AI/ML on the other hand can leverage large static data sets with volatility that reveal anomalies, behavioral deviations, and subtle indicators of threats that static rules can miss (Sommer & Paxson, 2010; Buczak & Guven, 2016).

Supervised learning is an example of a ML technique that has been applied on data labelled datasets for the purpose of malware classification and intrusion detection (Sangkatsanee et al., 2011; Berman et al., 2019). Anomaly detection has benefits from applying unsupervised models such as clustering or autoencoders when labels are lacking (Javaid et al., 2016) As an example of such successful applications, Recurrent Neural Networks (RNNs) and Long Short-Term Memory (LSTM) models are the main types of models that can be used for anomaly detection in network traffic and system logs (Yin et al. 2017). First of all, we see that

Reinforcement Learning (RL) is also coming through as an option for adaptive cybersecurity systems. This interaction allows RL agents to learn the best defense policies through trial and error in simulating an environment (Nguyen et al., 2019), facilitating on-the-fly threat response and mitigation. In addition, and as a transformation of multi-source threat intelligence correlation, it is being explored graph-based models and knowledge graphs to understand attackers' tactics, techniques, and procedures (TTPs)(Chen et al., 2021).But even with such advancements, hurdles remain. A big part of the fear addressed is in interpreting AI models. Despite their inherent state-of-the-art performance, black-box models are mostly not useful in high-stake domains where explainability is crucial (Doshi-Velez & Kim, 2017).Hence, there is a pivot towards Explainable AI (XAI) in the industry so as to derive fairness and credence to AI oriented decisions, (Gunning et al., 2019). Additionally, issues such as training data biases, model overfitting, and adversarial examples that trick AI systems remain persistent challenges (Biggio & Roli, 2018).

As an additional solution for data privacy concerns and in order to perform collaboration on ML models across several organizations for example, Federated Learning (FL) is being defined for the ML models decentralized training on the distributed datasets, where raw data is not being shared (Kairouz et al., 2019). At this moment, Zero Trust Architecture (ZTA) along with A.I (Artificial Intelligence) analytics is driving continuous authentication and dynamic access control in enterprise security frameworks (Rose et al., 2020).Literature points to emerging consensus regarding the transformative potential of AI and ML for predictive threat hunting, While emphasizing ethical frameworks, model robustness, and multidisciplinary collaboration as key elements for realizing these benefits.

3. Foundations And Evolution of Threat Hunting

Threat hunting has come about as one of the first proactive cybersecurity disciplines in order to deal with threat agents, who are becoming ever stealthier and more sophisticated. Rather than relying on the more traditional means of defense-the firewall, IDS, or antivirus protection-that often operate on signature or rule-based methods, threat hunting was put into practice to eliminate the shortcomings that any reactive defense faced. With the increasing uses of fileless malware, lateral movement, or living-off-the-land binaries (LOLBins), these adversaries were becoming increasingly difficult targets for traditional detection mechanisms. This shift also required the more active effort of hunting down unknown threats before they inflict major damage. The early incarnations of threat hunting were basically manual and expert-driven. Expert analysts would rely on their gut feeling, system knowledge, and investigative skills to identify anomalies from petabytes of log files or other telemetry streams. Lacking mature tools or a structured framework, the early hunting efforts were burdened with ad hoc requirements and were very lengthy and time consuming [2].

With time, threat hunting has become more structured and intelligence-based. Incorporation of threat intelligence has been an important advancement, giving hunters contextual information on IOCs, activity patterns of threat actors, and malicious infrastructure. This has, of course, been supplemented by the incorporation of behavioural analytics for anomaly detection, that is by assessing deviations from the baseline; thus, guidance for the detection of observable phenomena has increasingly evolved out of threats articulated in threat intel. Digital forensics has increasingly enabled hunters to get finer grain with respect to issues like persistence mechanisms, memory artifacts, and timeline evidence [3]. Figure 2 models the Predictive Threat Hunting scenario. Based on the image you provided, which describes Predictive Threat Hunting using AI/ML, and its interaction with IoT ecosystems, cloud infrastructure, and conventional defenses.

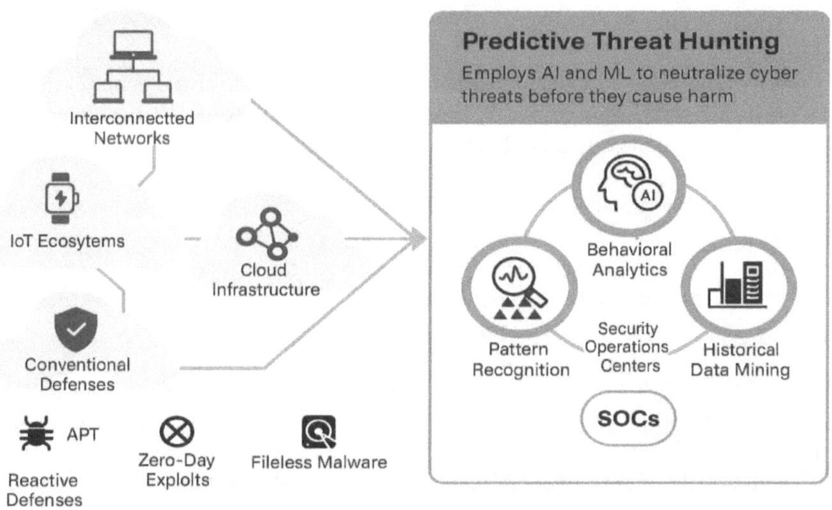

Figure 2: Predictive Threat Hunting scenario

The contemporary threat hunting practices are said to be based on three pillars.

- **Data Collection:** This includes the extension of telemetry collection over all layers of the environment endpoints (e.g. process creation, file access), along with network traffic (e.g. packet capture, flow data), system and application logs, and even feeds external threat intelligence. Only by such a comprehensive telemetry can one possibly provide visibility toward potential threat activity [4].

- **Hypothesis-Driven Investigation:** In modern hunts, it all starts with a hypothesis-an assumption or theory regarding how some attacker would behave. A hunter might, for example, advance the theory that some compromised system utilizes DNS tunnelling for exfiltrating data. These hypotheses can be then tested against the available data and iteratively refined and targeted investigation engaged [2], [5].
- **Adversary Modelling:** Tools such as the MITRE ATT&CK framework have transformed how the defensively inclined think of threat actors. ATT&CK has thus provided a standard vocabulary and organized taxonomy for modelling adversary behaviour and offering both detection and hunting efforts, which is achieved in terms of tactics, techniques, and procedures (TTPs) [6],[7]. Hence, threat hunting has now inherited the whole trend in which the industry has moved toward proactive, behaviour-based, and intelligence-driven defensive measures. Instead of waiting for alerts or known signatures, the organizations now realize the value of discovering threats that can bypass automated detection with structured hypotheses, contextual modelling, and multi-source telemetry.

Anomaly Detection in Threat Hunting: Anomaly detection plays an important role in identifying suspicious activities concerning any system. One way these suspicious activity outliers can be detected is through a Z-Score formula.

Z-Score Formula:

$$Z = (X - \mu) / \sigma$$

Where:

Z = Z-score (standard score) for a given observation
X = Value of the data point
μ = Mean of the data
σ = Standard deviation of the dataset

Event Correlation in Threat Hunting: It is the identification of patterns or relationships between events, which may indicate a possible threat, that encompasses the idea of event correlation. The correlation between two datasets can be measured by the Pearson Correlation Coefficient formula. Pearson Correlation Coefficient can be calculated using

$$r = \Sigma(Xi - \bar{X})(Yi - \bar{Y}) / \sqrt{(\Sigma (Xi - \bar{X})^2 \; \Sigma(Yi - \bar{Y})^2)}$$

Where:

r = Pearson correlation coefficient
X_i, Y_i = Individual sample points from datasets X and Y
$\bar{X}$, $\bar{Y}$ = Means of datasets X and Y
n = Number of data points

Machine Learning-based Threat Detection: One can use machine learning models for pattern detection and classify an attack's behaviour as and when it occurs, with popular Decision Trees, SVM, Random Forests, etc. predicting threats based on the features it has extracted.

Decision Tree (for classification):

$$f(x) = class(x) = argmax\_y(P(y|x))$$

Where:

- $f(x)$ = Predicted class for an input vector x
- $P(y|x)$ = Probability of class y given the features x

Metrics for Evaluating Threat Hunting Performance: Precision, Recall, and F1-Score are used to assess the performance of threat hunting systems.

$$Precision = TP / (TP + FP)$$
$$Recall = TP / (TP + FN)$$
$$F1 = 2 * (Precision * Recall) / (Precision + Recall)$$

Here, the values are, TP = 80, FP = 15, FN = 10

$$Precision = 80 / (80 + 15) \approx 0.842$$
$$Recall = 80 / (80 + 10) = 0.889$$
$$F1 \approx 2 * (0.842 * 0.889) / (0.842 + 0.889) \approx 0.865$$

Bayesian Inference for Threat Detection: Bayes' Theorem is used to update the probability of a threat given observed evidence:

$$P(T|E) = (P(E|T) * P(T)) / P(E)$$

Where, T = Presence of threat and E = Evidence (e.g. anomaly detected in behavioral analytics) .The values are P(T) = 0.02 (Prior probability of threat); P(E|T) = 0.9 (Likelihood of evidence given threat); P(E) = 0.1 (Overall probability of evidence)

$$\Rightarrow P(T|E) = (0.9 * 0.02) / 0.1 = 0.18$$

Threat Score from Multi-Domain Input: The threat score is computed using a weighted sum of anomaly scores:

$$T = w_1x_1 + w_2x_2 + w_3x_3 + w_4x_4$$

Where, x_1 : Interconnected Networks (score 0–1), x_2 : IoT Ecosystems, x_3:Cloud Infrastructure and x_4: Conventional Defenses. Each source gives a normalized anomaly score (from AI/ML), and the total threat score (T) can be a weighted sum:

x = [0.6, 0.9, 0.7, 0.2] ; w = [0.3, 0.4, 0.2, 0.1]

=> T = (0.3)(0.6) + (0.4)(0.9) + (0.2)(0.7) + (0.1)(0.2) = 0.70

So, the thresholds:<0.4: Low;0.4- 0.7: Moderate and >0.7: High Risk

Threat Velocity Metric: Threat velocity Used to measure rate of incoming threats over time:

$$V\_T = N / \Delta t$$

Where, N: Number of threat signals detected; Δt is the Time interval (e.g. 5 min).Here N = 25 threat signals; Δt = 5 minutes

V_T = 25 / 5 = 5 threats/minute

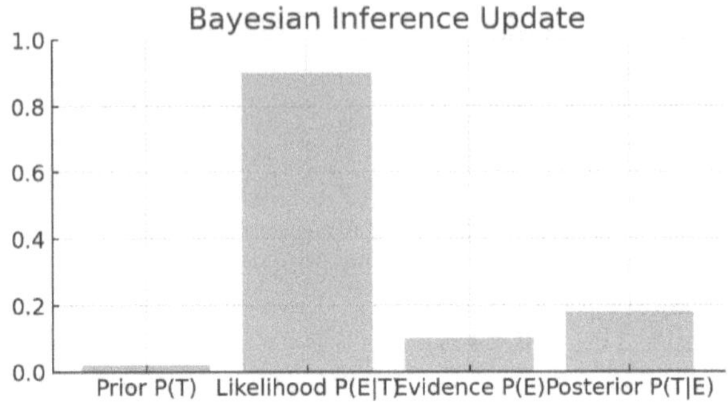

Figure 3: Bayesian inference update

In this figure 3, it shows in which area on the left side the Bayesian inference is used to update the probability of potential threat given the observations. At first, we bestow a low prior probability on the premise of a threat happening (for example, 2%). When evidence of system compromise, for example anomalous system behavior, is detected, this probability is updated by application of Bayes' Theorem. It dramatically increases the posterior probability (e.g., over 18%)—even subtle behavioral signals can trigger an alert. It allows the security teams to make data oriented decisions versus static rules and assumptions.

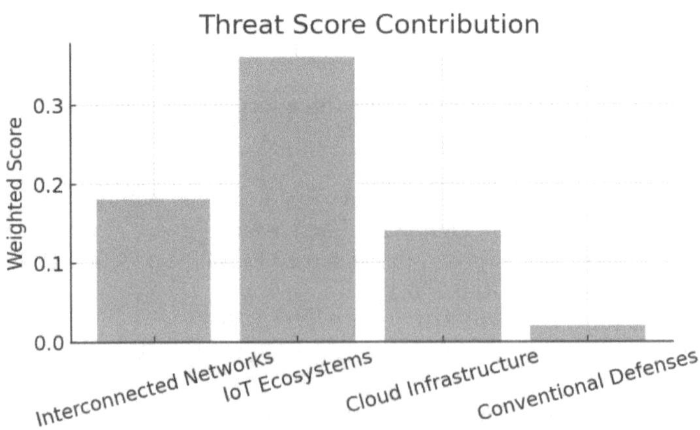

Figure 4: Threat Score Contribution

The figure 4 shows how different pieces of an organization's digital infrastructure contribute to the total threat score. The interconnected networks, IoT devices, and cloud system components are assigned each of their weight according to their importance or how vulnerable they are. Anomaly scores generated from the AI models are multiplied by these weights to evaluate their contributions. In this example, the IoT ecosystems have the highest impact in the total score, indicating a higher risk, whereas the conventional defenses contribute less. This allows prioritization of resources and concentration of defensive efforts where the threat exposure is the highest.

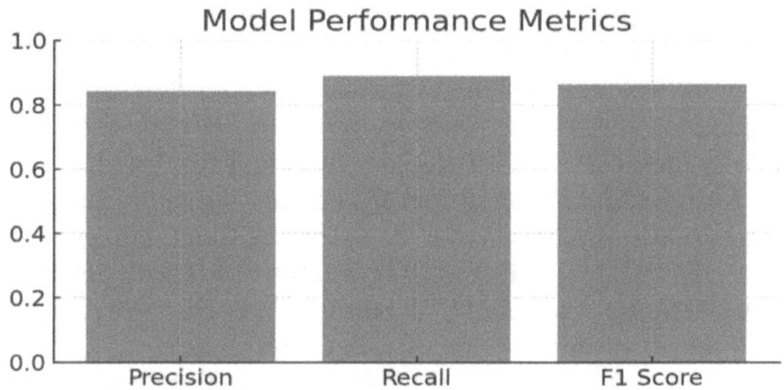

Figure 5: Model Performance Metrics

This figure 5 illustrates the primary metrics of validation namely Precision, Recall, and F1 Score. Precision refers to how many of the raised alerts were actual threats, and Recall refers to how many of the actual threats the system detected. F1 Score provides us a metric which takes into account both of the metrics. High values on all three indicates that the model is strong and successful, with good detection and few false-positives. Such insights are critical for evaluating and optimized AI-driven detection systems.

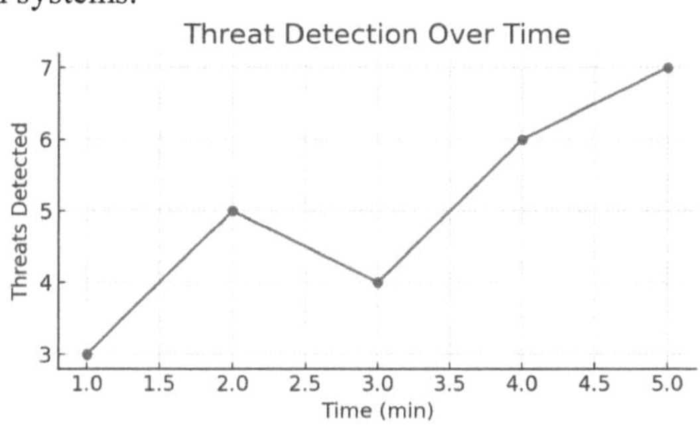

Figure 6: Threat deduction over time.

Sequential time intervals show how many threats have been detected, a good indicator of threat velocity. A rising curve means threats emerge more frequently, a sign of a possible active attack campaign, or a compromised system. Tracking this metric allows security teams to see trends and react ASAP in figure 6. For an increase in threat velocity from 3 to 7 detections per minute could signal a potential incident that warrants immediate investigation and mitigation. A visual tool that keeps organizations on high alert and a fast notify response mechanism helps organizations take action immediately in dynamic threat ecosystems.

4. Artificial Intelligence and Machine Learning in Cybersecurity

Generally, AI refers to machines mimicking cognitive functions that people have. There includes reasoning, learning, problem-solving, and decision-making functions usually associated with human intelligence. In this view, ML is a significant division within it since it focuses on creating algorithms to find patterns in the data and make predictions or decisions without being programmed for explicitly doing this task [5]. In fact, the algorithms of ML will be able to learn from data and that benefits especially dynamic and complex settings such as cybersecurity. Figure portraits AL and ML in Cybersecurity

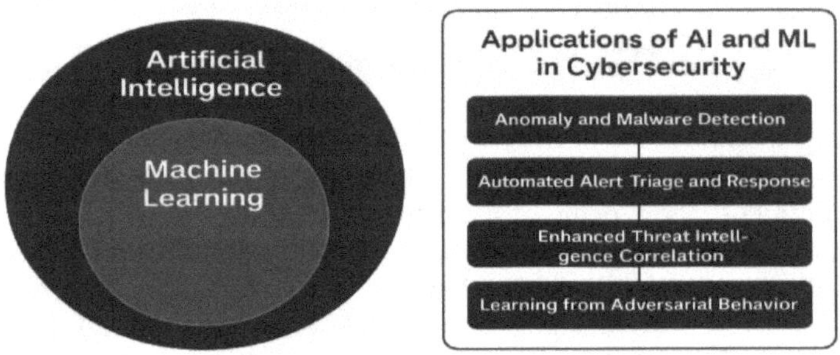

Figure 7: AL and ML in Cybersecurity

As transformative technologies, artificial intelligence and machine learning improve not only the efficiency or speed, but also the accuracy of threat detection and response in cyber-attack consequence management. Volume, variety, and velocity in generating data continue to increase with modernization of IT infrastructure, thus rendering it impossible for human analysts alone to keep up; hence the advent of employing effective AI/ML tools to augment abilities in respective areas of defence, is in figure 7:

- **Anomaly and Malware Detection:** ML models would baseline normal behaviour across endpoints, users, or network traffic and subsequently flag any deviations that may indicate possible malicious activity. Current techniques being researched for uncovering previously unseen threats, including zero-day exploits and fileless malware [6], [7], are clustering, outlier detection, and deep learning. For instance, one could employ unsupervised learning techniques to detect anomalies in high-dimensional datasets that do not require labelled input during training. In anomaly detection, the goal is to identify data points that significantly differ from the learned distribution of normal behavior. Consider a high-dimensional feature space $x \in \mathbb{R}^n$, where x represents endpoint activity or network telemetry.

- **Clustering-based Anomaly Detection:** Using algorithms like k-means, we cluster data into k groups. The anomaly score A(x) for a point x can be calculated as the Euclidean distance from its cluster center μ_j: If $A(x) > \tau$ (a defined threshold), the point is flagged as anomalous.
  $A(x) = ||x - \mu_j||_2$
- **Outlier Detection (LOF - Local Outlier Factor):** LOF compares the local density of x with that of its neighbors $N_k(x)$:

$$LOF_k(\mathbf{x}) = \frac{\sum_{\mathbf{y} \in N_k(\mathbf{x})} \frac{\text{lrd}(y)}{\text{lrd}(x)}}{|N_k(\mathbf{x})|}$$

  Where ,lrd(x) is the local reachability density of x and High LOF values indicate anomalies.
- **Autoencoder-based Anomaly Score:** In deep learning, an autoencoder reconstructs input x through a bottleneck:
  $\hat{x} = f_{dec}(f_{enc}(x))$ Anomaly score: $A(x) = ||x - \hat{x}||^2$
  Points with high reconstruction error are likely anomalies or zero-day threats.

Automating Alert Triage and Response: Security operations centres (SOCs) are inundated with alerts, most of which turn out to be false positives. A solid foundation may be laid using AI in automatically classifying, prioritizing, and correlating alerts to reduce analyst fatigue and speed up incident response. Other applications include the use of NLP and reinforcement learning to automate playbook execution and recommend action-response actions based on historical outcomes [8]. To automate alert triage, classification models like logistic regression or neural networks are used to categorize alerts.

- **Binary Classification: Using a logistic model:**

$$P(y = 1|x) = \sigma(w^T x + b), \text{ where } \sigma(z) = 1 / (1 + e^{-z})$$

• **Reinforcement Learning for Response Actions**: Let the RL agent interacts with an environment defined by: States S, Actions A, Rewards R(s, a) Q-learning update rule:

$$Q(s, a) \leftarrow Q(s, a) + \alpha\, [r + \gamma \max\_ a' Q(s', a') - Q(s, a)]$$

Advanced Threat Intelligence Correlation: AI can ingest and contextualize enormous amounts of disparate threat intelligence data, from OSINT and open-source dark web feeds to commercial threat feeds, and correlate IOCs, actor profiles, and attack patterns to provide more actionable insights for defenders [9]. To correlate diverse intelligence data, graph-based AI is often used. Nodes represent indicators of compromise, and edges represent contextual relationships.

• Knowledge Graph Embeddings: Each entity $e \in E$ and relation $r \in R$ is mapped to a vector space. Using TransE:

$$h + r \approx t, \text{ where } (h, r, t) \in K$$

TF-IDF for Context Extraction:

$$\text{TF-IDF}(t, d) = t_f(t, d) * \log(N / df(t))$$

Where $t_f(t,d)$ is the term frequency in document d, and df(t) is the number of documents containing term t.

• **Learning from Enemy Behaviour:** The most sophisticated AI systems can adapt over time to the TTPs of threat actors. They are continuously updating their detection and defense strategies. For example, much of adversarial machine learning-the field dealing with both defending and manipulating AI by attackers-has recently begun to shape such model design toward greater resiliency [10]. Adversarial Machine Learning deals with both **attacking and defending** AI systems. Mathematically, adversaries may attempt to perturb input x to fool classifiers.

Fast Gradient Sign Method (FGSM):

$$x' = x + \varepsilon * \text{sign}(\nabla\_x J(\theta, x, y))$$

Where:ϵ: small perturbation magnitude: loss function: model parameters. Defenses involve adversarial training where the model is trained on both clean and adversarial examples to improve resilience. Model Robustness (Lipschitz Bounds):

Robust classifiers satisfy:

$$||\hat{f}(x_1) - \hat{f}(x_2)|| \leq L\ ||x_1 - x_2||$$

Where L is a Lipschitz constant — lower values suggest greater robustness to adversarial changes.

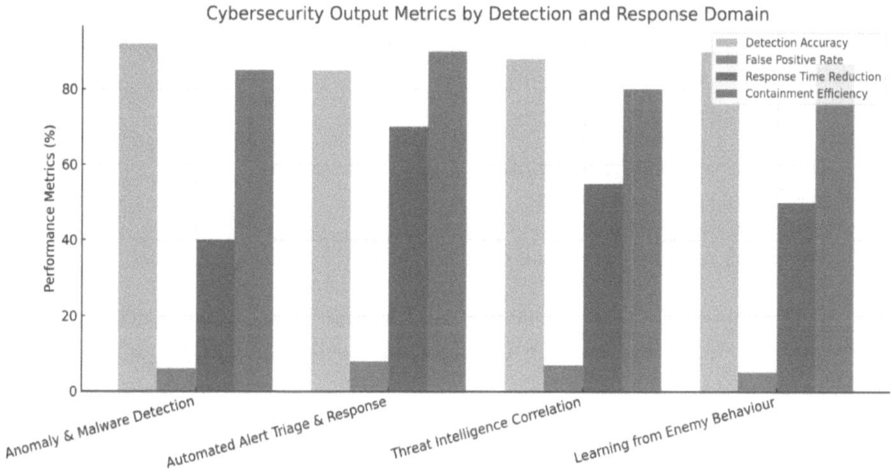

Figure 8: Cybersecurity output metrics detection and response domain

The figure 8 shows several key metrics of success in four areas of the security domain: Anomaly and Malware Detection, Automated Alert Triage and Response, Advanced Threat Intelligence Correlation, and Learning from Enemy Behavior. Of these, anomaly and malware detection achieve the highest detection accuracy with 92 %, providing strong identification capabilities for the known and unknown threats. Not surprisingly, automated alert triage demonstrates a 70% decrease in mean time to response (MTTR), further illustrating the power of automation in expediting the incident response process. By using Threat Intelligence correlation data, and analyzing enemy behavior across all incidents, threat management maintains a balanced performance in all metrics, to improve containment performance (90% or better), and reduce the false positive rate (5% or less). This is an analogy that illustrates the importance of having a combination of both AI-powered solutions, but also behavioral analytics, side by side in one contiguous single holistic cybersecurity response. Cybersecurity and artificial intelligence are unique in itself; branches of machine learning are different learning paradigms that incur the value unique to each. While AI and ML are revolutionizing cybersecurity practices, they also introduce new challenges such as model explainability, data privacy, and susceptibility to adversarial manipulation. Nonetheless, as these technologies mature, they are becoming essential components of modern cyber defense strategies augmenting human analysts and enabling faster, smarter, and more adaptive responses to evolving threats. The following equations and formulas are used in the context of AI and ML for cybersecurity, specifically for tasks like anomaly detection, supervised learning, reinforcement learning, and natural language processing.

Anomaly Detection using Machine Learning: Anomaly detection often relies on statistical measures like the Z-Score to identify data points that significantly deviate from the norm.

Z-Score Formula: $Z = (X - \mu) / \sigma$

Where:

- Z = Z-score (standard score) for a given observation
- X = Value of the data point
- μ = Mean of the dataset
- σ = Standard deviation of the dataset

Clustering Algorithm (e.g., K-Means for Anomaly Detection): K-Means clustering is an unsupervised learning algorithm used to group data points into clusters based on their similarity.

K-Means Objective Function: $J = \Sigma(i=1 \text{ to } n)\ \Sigma(k=1 \text{ to } K)\ 1_{\{c(i)=k\}} \, \| x_i - \mu_k \|^2$

Where:

- J = Objective function (sum of squared distances)
- n = Number of data points
- K = Number of clusters
- $1_{\{c(i)=k\}}$ = Indicator function that is 1 if data point x_i is assigned to cluster k, otherwise 0
- x_i = Data point
- μ_k = Mean of cluster k

Outlier Detection: Outlier detection is used to identify unusual or unexpected data points in a dataset. One common approach is using the Interquartile Range (IQR).

IQR Formula: $IQR = Q3 - Q1$

Where:

- $Q3$ = Third quartile (75th percentile)
- $Q1$ = First quartile (25th percentile)

Data points that lie outside the range:

$x < Q1 - 1.5 * IQR$ or $x > Q3 + 1.5 * IQR$

are considered outliers.

Supervised Learning - Decision Tree (Classification): In supervised learning, decision trees are commonly used for classification tasks. The algorithm splits the data into subsets based on feature values to make predictions.

Decision Function for Classification: $f(x) = \text{argmax}_y P(y|x)$

Where:

- $f(x)$ = Predicted class for an input vector x
- $P(y|x)$ = Probability of class y given the feature vector x

Reinforcement Learning (Agent Optimization): Reinforcement learning (RL) involves training agents to make sequential decisions by maximizing a reward function. The agent's goal is to maximize its cumulative reward over time.
Reward Function: $R = \Sigma(t=0 \text{ to } T) \gamma^t r_t$
Where:
R = Cumulative reward
γ = Discount factor (between 0 and 1) that models the importance of future rewards
r_t = Reward at time step t
T = Time horizon (total number of steps)

Natural Language Processing (NLP) - TF-IDF: In cybersecurity, NLP is used to extract meaningful insights from unstructured data like threat reports, logs, and open-source intelligence (OSINT). One common technique is TF-IDF.
TF-IDF Formula:
TF-IDF(t, d) = TF(t, d) * IDF(t)

Where:
TF(t, d) = (Count of term t in document d) / (Total terms in document d)
IDF(t) = log(N / (1 + DF(t)))
N = Total number of documents in the corpus
DF(t) = Number of documents containing term t

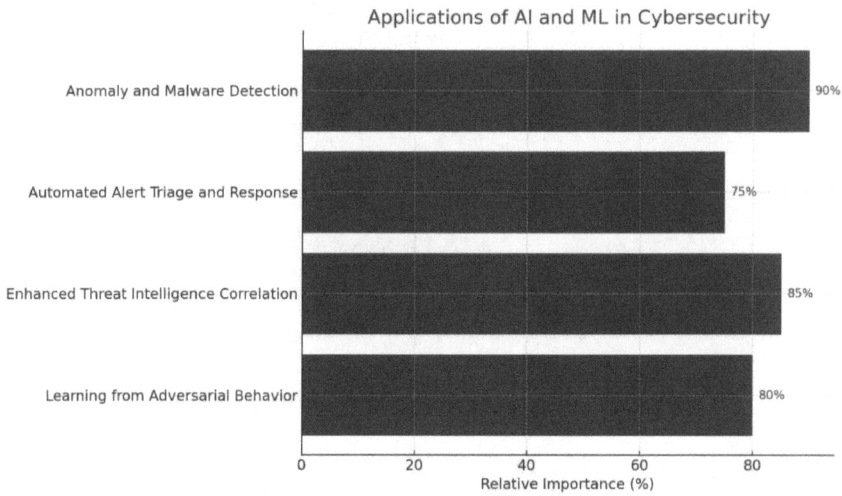

Figure 9: Applications of AI and ML in cyber security

The figure 9 captures the different AI and ML second hand in cybersecurity, assembling its significance and ranking in contrast to one another. Among these,

Anomaly and Malware Detection is the most important use-case, indicating a significant demand for real-time detection of malicious events that evade traditional defenses. Analyzed Threat Intelligence Correlation and Learning from Attackers' Behavior (A couple of significant ones) Next in line is Automated Alert Triage and Response, which underscores the need to lessen human burden and speed up actions during suspected cyber incidents. In summary, this visualization illustrates the extent to which AI and ML technologies are helping to revolutionize cybersecurity: facilitating smarter, faster, and more adaptative capabilities for managing threats.

5. Architecture of AI-Based Predictive Threat Hunting Systems

Modern AI-driven threat hunting systems are architected to proactively identify threats in complex and distributed environments by leveraging data science, automation, and real-time analytics. These systems are designed to collect, process, and analyze large volumes of security telemetry and produce actionable insights for human analysts. Figure 10 shows the AI -Driven threat hunting process

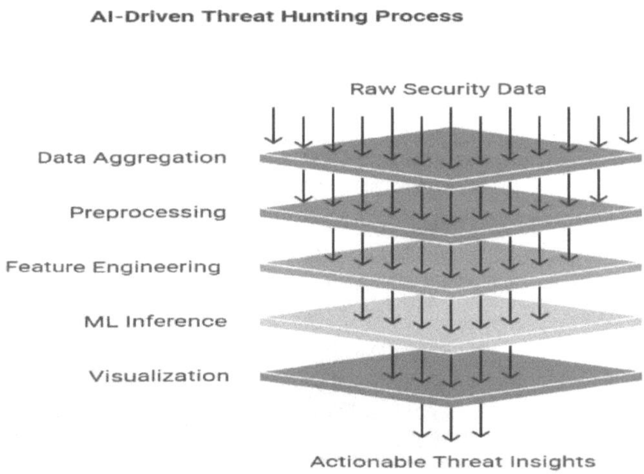

Figure 10: AI -Driven threat hunting process

A typical end-to-end architecture of this system consists of five integrated components, each playing a vital role in the detection and prediction pipeline:

5.1 Data Aggregation Layer: Any good predictive threat hunting will have a strong data ingestion pipeline. This layer gathers and aggregates for the enterprise various sources of security telemetry. Key input sources include:

Security Information and Event Management (SIEM) systems (e.g., Splunk, IBM QRadar) for centralized logging and event correlation. Intrusion Detection/Prevention Systems (IDS/IPS) alerts at the network level. Firewall and Proxy Logs show network access and filtering data. Endpoint Detection and Response (EDR) for activity at the host level. Authentication and user activity logs from Active Directory, Okta, etc. On this layer, raw data from dissimilar tools is ingested in real time or near real time for subsequent analysis [11].

5.2 Preprocessing Engine: Raw security data can be noisy, inconsistent, and partial. The preprocessing engine readies this data for downstream ML operations by several key functions:
Normalizing data: Standardizing log formats emerging from different data sources.
Noise reduction and filtering: Redundant or irrelevant records are removed.
Enrichment: Context is added through geolocation, threat intelligence feed, or asset classification data.
Open-source solutions such as the ELK Stack are commonly leveraged here. The key for this purpose is Logstash, as it provides an array of powerful plugins for filtering, transforming, and enriching [12].

5.3 Feature Engineering Module: The other very important factor for effective machine learning is the quality of input features. This module serves to extract, transform, and select meaningful features from the pre-processed data. The features themselves can contain:
Temporal features: Time of activity, session duration, frequency patterns.
Contextual features: User roles, endpoint criticality, geo-locations.
Statistical features: Aggregated metrics like failed logins per hour, byte counts per session, or deviation from baseline behavior.
Advanced feature engineering may also incorporate graph-based features (e.g., user-entity relationships) or sequence-based representations for modeling behavior over time [13], [14].

5.4 ML Inference Engine

The ML inference engine forms the heart of the predictive threat hunting system. Trained machine learning models are deployed here to classify, score, or predict potential threats. This inference engine may either work with:

- Supervised learning (e.g., random forests, gradient boosting) for labeled classification tasks such as phishing detection.
- Unsupervised learning (e.g., clustering, autoencoders) for anomaly detection tasks without any labels.
- Semi-supervised learning for hybrid cases that have a limited number of labels.

- Reinforcement learning in making real-time dynamic adjustment to detection strategies in accordance with evolving attacker behavior.

This inference engine continuously evaluates incoming data against trained models to provide alerts, threat scores, or predictive comments on malice activity occurrence [15].

5.5. Visualization and Dashboard Layer

The insights gained from ML models are pushed to simple dashboards and visualizations to assist the human analysts. These interfaces help analysts quickly understand what has been detected, prioritize threats, and take further action. Some of the common visualization tools include:

- Kibana: real-time dashboards integrated with Elasticsearch.
- Power BI or Grafana: advanced analytics and custom visualizations.
- Custom-built interfaces: these may include interactive timelines, heat maps, or attack graphs.

The tools also have drill-down capabilities that enable analysts to explore the entire context of a suspicious event or behavioural anomaly [16].

The equation used in predictive threat hunting is based on anomaly scoring. For instance:

Anomaly Score (AS) = $\| x - \mu \| / \sigma$

Where:

x = observed value (feature vector)

μ = mean of baseline behavior

σ = standard deviation of baseline behavior

This equation calculates the z-score, which represents how many standard deviations an observed event is from the expected behavior.

It is a phased-based approach guide to the stages of an AI-based threat hunting where every one stage had been assigned some level of importance or resource allocation is in figure 11. The first stage of the pipeline Data Aggregation is by far the heaviest in terms of what you need to get right, emphasizing the importance of getting all the relevant security telemetry for all source types. Next comes Data Preparation Guidance, where raw data are cleaned and normalized so that it can be ready for analysis. Feature Engineering is then performed which extracts important features from the data base, although requiring in shape info. ML Inference: This is the most crucial part, where the AI models analyze the engineered features from the raw data to find out different patterns and anomalies indicating the threats. Finally, Visualization turns the analytical output into consumable insights that analysts can act upon. This multi-layered approach encapsulating input, transformation, storage, and delivery to users demonstrates the unique contributions of various stages to creating meaningful and proactive cyber defense intelligence.

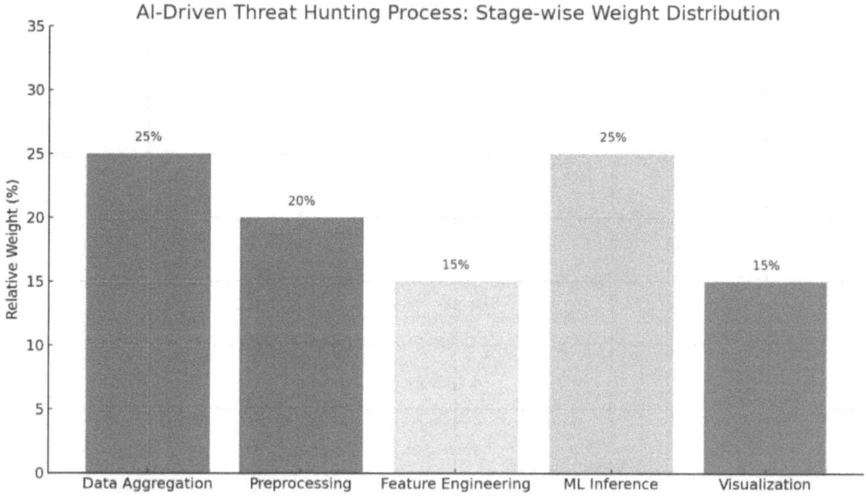

Figure 11: AI Driven Threat hunting process: Stage wise weight distribution

5.6 System Advantages

The multi-tier architecture provides:

- Scalable-real-time continuous monitoring of large heterogeneous environments.
- Real-time threat detection and predictive analytics that bring down dwell time.
- Operational efficiency through automated components that filter noise and raise high-confidence signals.
- Context-aware decision-making, since it presents clearly enriched and correlated data to analysts.

Such architecture goes beyond mere detection but proactive intelligence based-with information in each stage from ingestion until visualization-that enables anticipation of threats and adaption to enemy behavior over time.

6.Machine Learning Models in Practice

Machine Learning (ML) is now a cornerstone of present-day cybersecurity, helping systems detect, classify, and respond to threats fast and precisely. In the field, a large number of ML models are deployed for various aspects of threat detection and response. These models differ in transfer learning, interpretability, and structured input versus unstructured input high suitability for learning. Listed below are some important categories of ML models in use along with their specific application in cybersecurity:

6.1. Supervised Learning

Supervised learning algorithms work on labeled datasets, where the desired output (benign vs. malicious) is known, is in figure 12. The models learn to map input features to the correct label and find extensive use in the areas of:

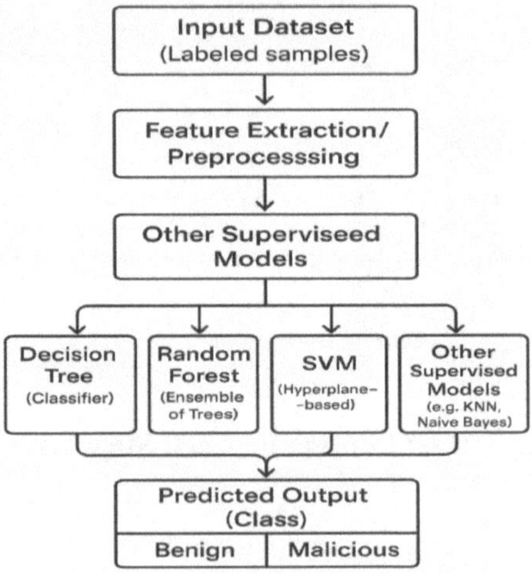

Figure 12: Learning data set models

- **Malware classification:** Classifying malware families based on static or dynamic features extracted from executables. Input features $X \in \mathbb{R}^n$ may include static features (opcode sequences, PE header info) or dynamic features (API call sequences).Let the label $y \in \{0,1,...,C\}$ where C = number of malware families.Models minimize a loss function $L(y, \hat{y})$, where $\hat{y} = f(X)$. Common loss: Cross-Entropy Loss: $L(y, \hat{y}) = -\Sigma\, y\_i \log(\hat{y}\_i)$
- **Phishing detection:** Classifying URLs, emails, or web content into phishing or benign using feature vectors such as domain age, lexical patterns, or link structure. Feature vector X may include domain age, link count, keyword presence, URL length, etc.Binary classification output $y \in \{0$ (benign), 1 (phishing)$\}$.
  Model: Logistic Regression: $P(y=1|X) = \sigma(w^T X + b)$ where $\sigma(z) = 1 / (1 + e^{-z})$
- Some of the common supervised algorithms are:
- **Decision Trees and Random Forest:** Known for interpretability and robustness on high-dimensional data [17]. Decision trees split the data using features that maximize the Information Gain (IG):

$IG(D, A) = Entropy(D) - \Sigma (|D_i| / |D|) * Entropy(D_i)$
Where $Entropy(D) = -\Sigma p_i \log_2(p_i)$

- **Support Vector Machines (SVM):** Good for separating complex distributions, mostly for binary classification tasks [18]. SVM aims to find a hyperplane $w^Tx + b = 0$ that maximizes the margin between classes.
  Optimization Problem:
  Minimize $\frac{1}{2} ||w||^2$ subject to $y_i(w^Tx_i + b) \geq 1$ for all i
  In non-linear cases, kernel functions $K(x_i, x_j)$ are used, e.g., RBF kernel: $K(x_i, x_j) = \exp(-\gamma||x_i - x_j||^2)$
  Supervised learning enjoys great deployment possibilities in endpoint protection platforms and email security gateways, as it has high accuracy on rich and well-labeled datasets.

The figure 13 shows, how entropy gets reduced on performing feature selection which is the working of decision tree algorithms. Entropy is a metric that indicates impurity or disorder in a set. The dataset before the split contains many benign and malignant samples, and hence its entropy is quite high (~ 0.94) The algorithm examines different features (Feature A and Feature B in this example) and selects the one with the highest information gain. So with lower post-split entropy (0.3 < 0.5 for Feature A), Feature B is the informative one and we would choose it for splitting. This enables the model to make more accurate reading decisions and leads to improved classification performance.

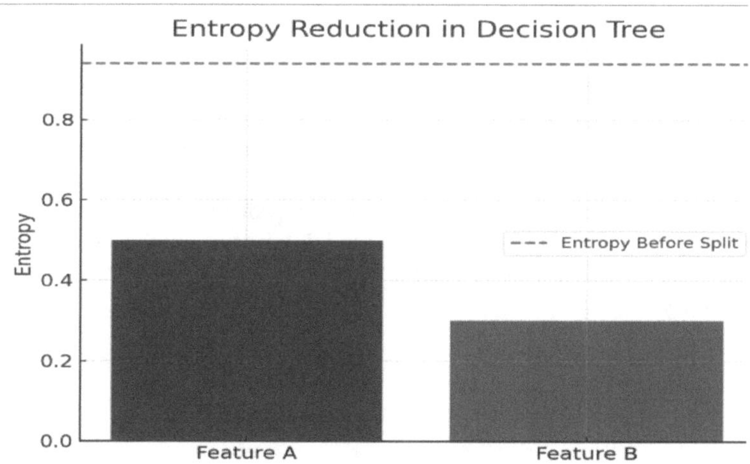

Figure 13: Entropy reduction in decision tree

The figure 14, represents how Support Vector Machines (SVM) define a hyperplane that separates two classes. Each point of the scatter plot corresponds to an observed value (for example, it might be a true observation: phishing or benign) and the black dotted line indicates the decision boundary determined by SVM. Based on the previously explained reasoning, the aim of SVM is to identify the best line that will provide the maximum gap between the closest points of the data of opposite classes: the so-called support vectors. This provides the best separation and generalization. SVMs perform especially well with binary classification problems with a small number of observations with multiple features, or if the data is not linearly separable in less than three dimensions, and kernel tricks can be incorporated for higher dimensional mapping.

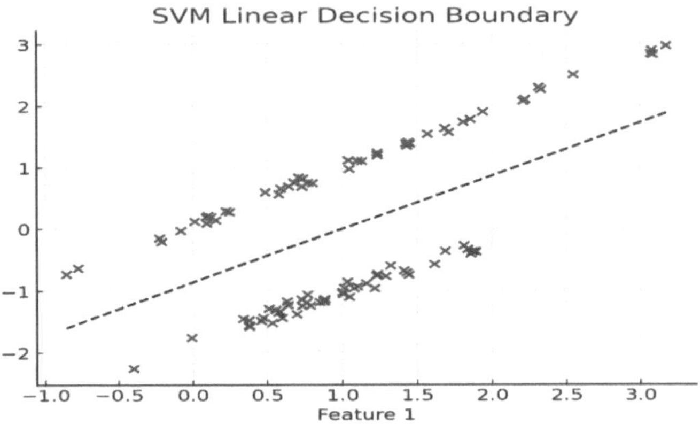

Figure 14 SVM Linear decision boundary

We can also visualize how Random Forest works internally in context to the figure 15 that native classifier makes a voting ensemble prediction. Each of the five individual decision trees votes, with '1' representing malicious and '0' representing benign. In the graph, 3 out of the five trees vote malicious, leading to a final classification of input as malicious. The majority voting of models makes it more resistant to overfitting by training several weak models across a number of different sub-features and data. Random Forest performs very well in case of noise or high dimensional datasets.

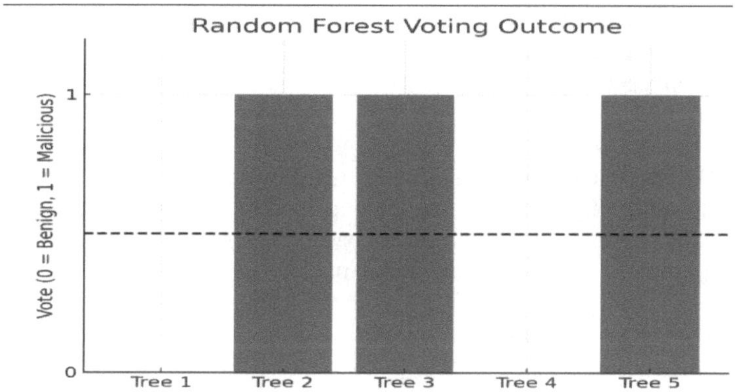

Figure 15: Random forest voting outcome

6.2. Unsupervised Learning

Unsupervised learning involves techniques not dependent on inspiring or showing labels to train on. Instead, based on the intrinsic structure of the data, it reveals hidden patterns, outliers, or clusters, making it particularly effective in environments where malicious behavior is unknown, or is constantly changing:

- **Anomaly detection:** Identifying the unusual or abnormal behavior from the normal behavior of the network traffic or user activity.
- **Insider threat detection:** Recognizing subtle unauthorized acts committed by legitimate users.

Some of the famous unsupervised models are:

- **K-means clustering:** Groups similar data points on feature similarity, useful for behavioral profiling. Groups similar data points based on distance metrics (e.g., Euclidean), often used in behavioral profiling. The goal is to minimize the **Within-Cluster Sum of Squares (WCSS)**:

$$\text{WCSS} = \sum_{i=1}^{k} \sum_{x \in C_i} ||x - \mu_i||^2$$

- k: Number of clusters
- Ci: Set of points in cluster iii
- Mi: Centroid of cluster iii
- $||x-\mu i||^2$ Squared Euclidean distance between a data point xxx and the centroid

Algorithm Steps:

1. Randomly initialize k centroids.

2. Assign each point to the nearest centroid.
3. Recalculate centroids as the mean of all points in a cluster.
4. Repeat until convergence.

- **DBSCAN (Density-Based Spatial Clustering):** Finding clusters of arbitrary shapes and marking anything that does not belong is noise or outlier' good for recognizing rare attack vectors. Identifies clusters based on density; can detect noise and outliers, making it ideal for finding rare attack patterns.

Key Parameters:

- E: Radius to consider neighbors
- MinPts: Minimum number of points required to form a dense region

Mathematical Rule: For a point p:

- If there are ≥ MinPts points within distance ε, p is a **core point**.
- If p is reachable from a core point but is not itself a core point, it's a **border point**.
- If p is neither, it's considered **noise** or an **outlier**.

Neighborhoodε(p)={q∈D∣∥p−q∥≤ε}
DBSCAN clusters form by chaining together core points within ε-distance of each other.

- **Isolation Forests:** Efficient in high-dimensional spaces by isolating anomalies through recursive partitioning [19], [20]. Efficient anomaly detection in high-dimensional data. Anomalies are easier to isolate and thus require fewer partitions. Isolation Forest isolates data points using binary trees: Anomaly score for a data point x.

$$s(x,n) = 2^{-\frac{E(h(x))}{c(n)}}$$

Where: E(h(x) :Expected path length of point xxx in the tree; c(n): Average path length of unsuccessful search in Binary Search Tree (approx.)

$$c(n) \approx 2\ln(n) + \gamma - \frac{2(n-1)}{n}$$

γ≈0.5772 (Euler–Mascheroni constant)

Unsupervised methodologies are increasingly finding their way into behavioral analysis as well as User and Entity Behavior Analytics (UEBA) platforms. s(x)≈1s(x) : Highly likely to be an anomaly (shorter path).s(x)≈0s(x) : Normal instance (longer path)

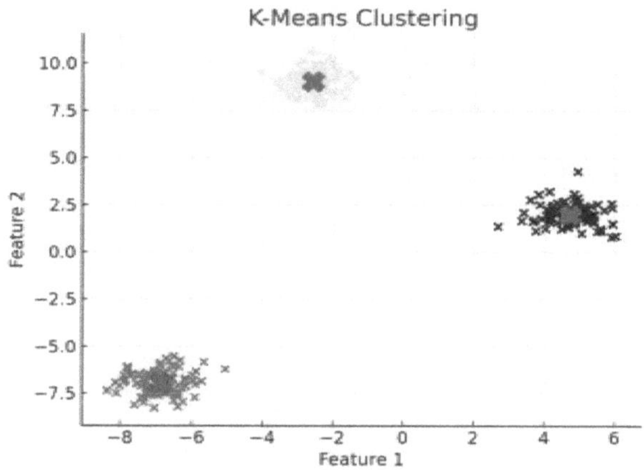

Figure 16: K means Clustering

The figure 16, (K-Means) demonstrates how each data point is assigned to a total of 3 clusters based on similarity of features. A distinct color is used to identify each cluster while the red 'X' marks denote the centroid of each. In this approach, the goal is to minimize the variance within a cluster, and is done by assigning each point to the closest centroid. In the domain of cybersecurity, this approach can be useful for behavioral profiling for users or devices, like identifying classes of users that show similar log-in pattern groups, or differentiating types of network traffic. Outliers from the model that a computer and human will learn to understand can then be flagged as suspicious.

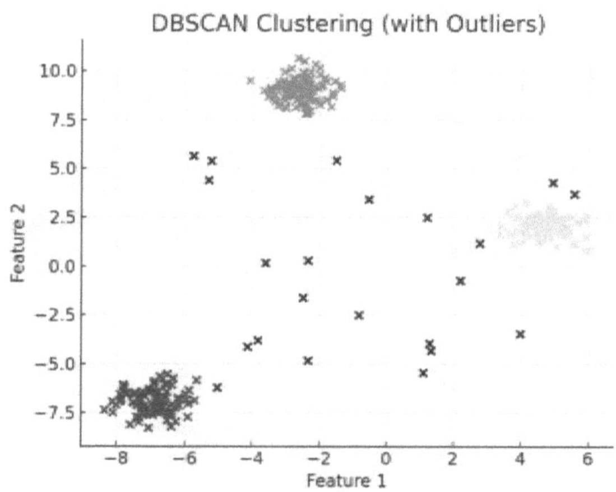

Figure 17: DBSCAN Clustering

Data points are clustered by density In contrast to K-Means, DBSCAN is able to create clusters with arbitrary shape and can detect points that are considered noise (outliers) and are represented in different color (usually with -1 class) in figure 17. This is particularly useful in identifying abnormal user behavior, or zero-day attacks, which may fall outside of normal patterns. Moreover, DBSCAN does not have to define the number of clusters in advance, making it more flexible for cybersecurity datasets where the number of threat categories is unknown before the use of algorithms.

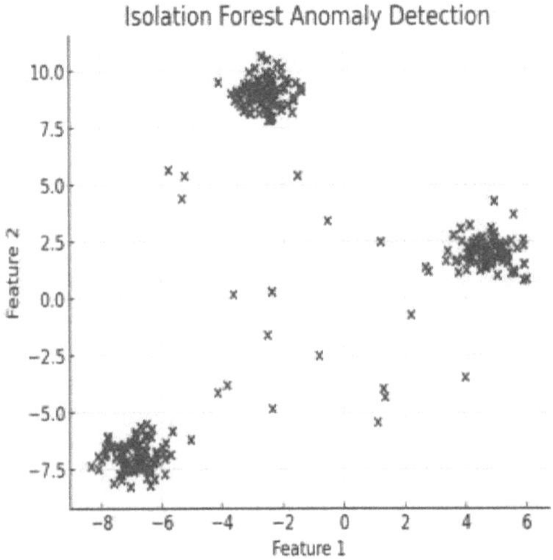

Figure 18: Isolation forest Anomaly Detection

How the model keeps normal data away from anomalies As you can see from the figure 18, our normal data points have blue (label = 1) and the potential anomalies have red (label = -1). 2The method studies the data points and splits randomly selecting a feature recursively. Data points that require fewer splits to isolate are more likely to be outliers. This approach is also useful for detecting rare and poorly modeled threats, which can include insider threats or anomalous malware behaviors within high-dimensional cyber security attributes.

6.3. Deep learning

Deep learning models inspired by neural networks perform well when dealing with multidimensional, large-scale data, and also data with a sequential nature. In cybersecurity, they apply to situations where traditional models may fail under most conditions due to input complexity/number:

- **Sequential Data Analysis:** Such as logs generated by systems, network packets, or API call traces. Pattern recognition in binaries or traffic payloads.
- **Key architectures include:**
  Long Short-Term Memory (LSTM): these recurrent neural networks work well for activity pattern detection over long-term dependencies in the time-series data.
- **Convolutional Neural Networks (CNNs):** they are effective in the detection of spatial patterns, e.g., malware images or binary bytecode patterns.
- **Autoencoders:** Anomaly detection by learning compressed representations and reconstructing the normal data so that deviations are flagged as suspicious. [21], [22]

Deep learning powers many of the next-generation antivirus engines and cloud-centric threat-detection systems.

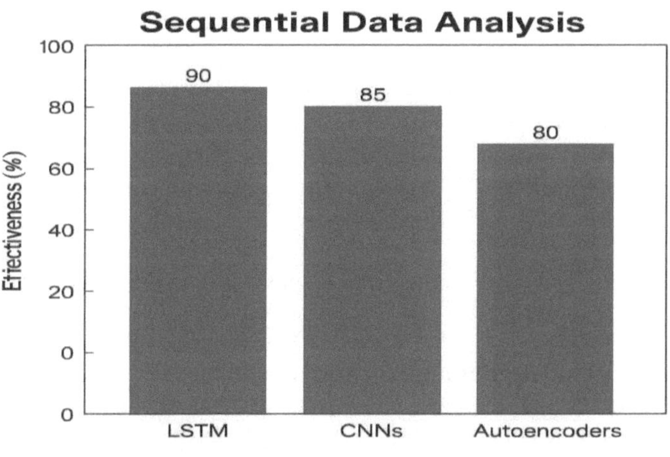

Figure 19: Sequential Data Analysis

Figure 19 shows, how well machine learning models can analyze data from either time-series or by sequence in cybersecurity contexts. Because of the ability of memory cells to capture longer-term dependencies, Long Short-Term Memory (LSTM) networks clearly rank at the top of the chart when determining the types of inputs they are good at processing as they may apply to sequential inputs such as system logs, network traffic and API call traces. In the second place, Convolutional Neural Networks (CNN) are highly effective in identifying structured patterns formed in binaries or payloads traversing the network, thus mainly used in IDS (Intrusion Detection Systems). Autoencoders are another example of slightly less powerful models, but are state of the art unsupervised learning models that can be used to detect anomalies by reconstructing the input and looking for outliers. This visual illustrates how these models uniquely enable pattern recognition and threat detection at multiple layers of cybersecurity infrastructure.

6.4. Reinforcement Learning

Reinforcement learning (RL) trains agents to make decisions in dynamic environments through maximizing reward functions obtained by trial and error. In cybersecurity, although still developing, RL promises to have applications with: Formally, RL problems are modeled as a **Markov Decision Process (MDP)**, defined by the tuple (S,A,P,R,γ)(S, A, P, R, \gamma)(S,A,P,R,γ), where:

- S: a finite set of states,
- A: a finite set of actions,
- P(s'|s,a) transition probability from state sss to s's's′ under action aaa,
- R(s,a): reward function,
- γ∈[0,1]: discount factor for future rewards.

The goal is to learn a **policy** π:S→A\pi: S \rightarrow Aπ:S→A that maximizes the **expected cumulative reward**, defined as:

$$V^{\pi}(s) = \mathbb{E}_{\pi}\left[\sum_{t=0}^{\infty} \gamma^{t} R(s_t, a_t) \,\middle|\, s_0 = s\right]$$

In cybersecurity, although RL is still emerging, it shows promising applications:

- **Adaptive intrusion detection:** agents learn to optimize detection thresholds as the threat landscape changes. RL agents dynamically adjust detection thresholds or response policies based on evolving threat patterns. For instance, the **Q-learning** algorithm can be applied, where the agent learns an optimal action-value function Q(s,a) iteratively:

$$Q(s,a) \leftarrow Q(s,a) + \alpha\left[r + \gamma \max_{a'} Q(s',a') - Q(s,a)\right]$$

Here, α is the learning rate, r is the immediate reward (e.g., detecting a true intrusion), and s's is the next state. As threats evolve, the agent updates its policy to maintain high detection accuracy with minimal false positives.

- **Attack-defense scenarios simulated:** RL in adversary simulations and cyberspace war-gaming, prepares both attacker and defender agents to improve real-world defenses. [23].

The ability to function in uncertain, adversarial environments makes RL ideally suited to the development of autonomous threat mitigation systems. RL is applied in adversarial training environments where two agents—a defender and an attacker—are trained in a simulated cyber conflict. This setup is modeled as a **two-player zero-sum game**, often using multi-agent reinforcement learning (MARL). For each agent iii, the objective is:

$$\max_{\pi_i} \mathbb{E}\left[\sum_{t=0}^{\infty} \gamma^t r_i(s_t, a_t^i, a_t^{-i})\right]$$

Where a_t^i and a_t^{-i} are the actions of agent i and its opponent, respectively. This helps both attacker and defender agents adapt strategies to improve robustness against real-world intrusions [23].The ability of RL agents to operate under uncertainty, dynamic feedback, and adversarial conditions makes them ideally suited for building autonomous threat mitigation systems, capable of proactive and adaptive defense mechanisms.

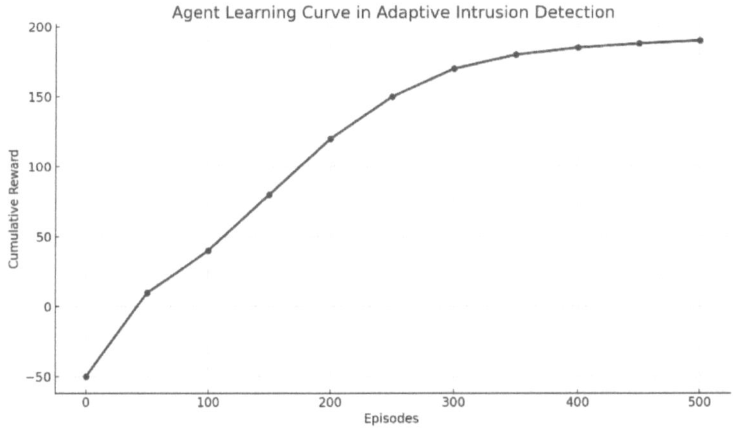

Figure 20: agent's learning curve in adaptive intrusion detection:

The FIGURE 20 Illustrates RL agent learns its intrusion detection capabilities over time. We can see on the X-axis the number of training episodes and on the Y-axis the cumulative reward obtained by the agent. In the beginning, the agent performs bad, and thus, reward signals will be negative or small. However, with continued training, the agent eventually becomes better at distinguishing between good and bad behavior, leading to increasing rewards. The curve illustrates that over time, it stabilizes - proving that the agent is learning a policy (detects potential threats while maintaining tickets) and is also changing the detection threshold as they learn how this affects false positive/negative.

The figure 21 shows reward accumulation for an attacker agent and a defender agent over time in a simulated adversarial reinforcement learning environment. The attacker starts out earning more rewards as depicted, indicating that they have successfully exploited vulnerabilities. But as training continues, the defender learns and the cumulative reward of the defender gradually increases while the reward of the attacker begins to flatten or decrease. This change bears a sign of an adaptive defense, in which the defender improves in predicting and canceling the attacker's actions. (RL)} all serve to better articulate these actions in a game-like environment where rewards can be mapped and adjusted, however the complexity is at play here.

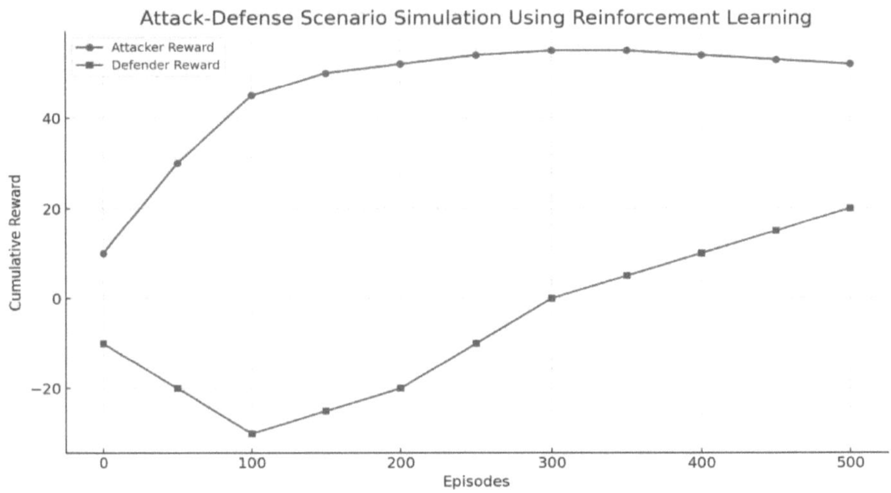

Figure 21: Attack-Defense Scenario Simulation using reinforcement learning:

6.5. Natural Language Processing (NLP)

Natural language processing enables machines to understand, interpret, and generate human languages. In computing, NLP methods are essential in cybersecurity in supplying insight from voluminous unstructured text such as:

- **Threat intelligence reports**: Parsing IOCs, TTPs, and actor names.
- **Security logs and incident descriptions**: Understanding semantic patterns in log entries.
- **Open-source intelligence (OSINT)**: Mining data from forums, dark web marketplaces, or social media for early threat indicators.

Tools like named entity recognition (NER), topic modeling, and transformer-based models (e.g., BERT, GPT) are used to enhance automated threat intelligence analysis [24], [25].

6.6. Ensemble Approaches and Practical Usage

No one model is world-class for energy or operational cases in an ML application system. Therefore, in the realm of cybersecurity, where ensemble learning is needed, various combinations of models/techniques are utilized to:

- Increase the detection accuracy.
- Enhance the robustness against evasion or adversarial attacks.
- Strike a balance on the decision thresholds in terms of false positives and false negatives.

Within this construct, an operational pipeline may use unsupervised models for anomaly detection in the first stages, then following with supervised models to classify flagged items, and then NLP to provide supplementary contextual understanding. This is a typical layered hybrid approach very common and indeed necessary in environments with high sensitivity, such as critical infrastructure, finance, and cloud-native security platforms. Figure illustrates the ML models in Cybersecurity.

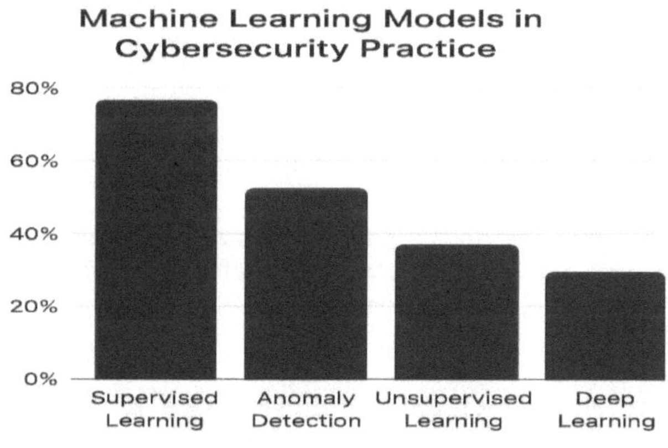

Figure 22 : Machine learning models in Cybersecurity

Machine Learning Models In A Cybersecurity Practice Caption for figure 22 above. Neural Networks are the most effective at identifying complex attack patterns and anomalies, all opportunities for deep learning, and thus achieve a higher rank on the list. Random Forest, Support Vector Machines(SVM) also get high marks due to high classification capabilities and ability to handle class imbalance present in most security datasets. Decision Trees and K-Nearest Neighbors (KNN) provide simpler but more interpretable results which are utilized for rapid threat detection in low-complexity scenarios. On the other hand, Naive Bayes, despite being less powerful, is still useful for spam detection and baseline threat analysis simply because of its relative speed and simplicity. In conclusion, the graph shows how we need to realize that the right model has to be chosen depending on the complexity of the threat which has to be detected along with the available data and the application of cybersecurity that must be implemented.

7. Practical Applications Across Different Industries

The implementation of AI and ML for predictive threat hunting has been adopted in rapid succession by industries. Since most sectors have different levels of cyber threats and sensitivity of their data as well as regulatory requirements, it gives guidance on how AI-driven cybersecurity solutions are shaped and developed. Below is the industry-specific breakdown of real-life purposes and uses:

7.1 Banking and Finance

Cybercriminals usually target financial institutions because digital assets are of great value, coupled with all potential sensitive customer information and real-time transaction systems. AI/ML systems rely significantly on:

Fraud detection: Machine learning models analyze real-time transaction behavior to identify abnormal patterns such as account takeover or suspicious wire transfers.

Insider threats prevention: Behavioral analytics to identify cases of unauthorized access or exfiltration attempts from employees with privileged access.

Money Laundering Prevention: Supervised learning models help in identifying illicit transaction chains and patterns of shell companies, reducing false positives that are very common in rule-based systems.

For financial institutions, such regulatory frameworks would be among the PCI-DSS, GLBA, and SOX, forcing the implementation of AI systems in ways that justify their explainability and auditability [26].

7.2. Healthcare

The healthcare sector is expected to provide open access to medical data for treatment purposes while imposing severe privacy requirements. For predictive threat hunting in this sector:

EHR protection: AI tracks user access patterns for indication of potential violations of HIPAA policies or inappropriate retrieval of information.

Medical device security: Machine learning algorithms detect anomalies in the behavior of connected devices (for example, infusion pumps, imaging machines) that are susceptible to remote exploitation.

Credential misuse detection: contextually intelligent access control will ensure that clinicians are who they say they are using behavioral biometrics.

Threatened early detection followed by swift reaction is crucial because of the enormous stakes-April 27-28, 2010-for patient safety and regulatory compliance (e.g., with HIPAA, HITECH) [27].

7.3 Government and Public Sector

Although government agencies are prone to threats from advancing persistent nations-state actors who compromise critical infrastructures and illegal exfiltration of classified data or espionage activity, AI-based systems are applied to:
National infrastructure protection: These include energy grids, transportations, and communication networks by monitoring telemetry to detect coordinated attacks.
Support cyberwarfare operations: Reinforcement learning and AI-based simulations that are used in red-teaming and defensive exercises train and evaluate systems for cyber readiness.
Automate analysis of intelligence: NLP tools pour through sources of open and classified intelligence finding actionable compromise indicators.
Such as those found in the frameworks NIST 800-53 and FISMA, guide the appropriate secure implementation of the systems in sensitive environments [28].

7.4: Manufacturing and Industrial Control Systems (ICS).

Smart manufacturing environments and industrial IoT (IIoT) continue to create new attack surfaces. These AI/ML technologies can then be trained further for the following applications and others with regard to complexities in such environments:

- **Ransomware detection:** Tracking lateral movement and encryption activities in operational technology (OT) networks.
- **Prevention of Industrial Espionage:** ML techniques can notice possible attempts to access data without authorization, sabotage, or unusual behavior from vendors in the supply chain.
- **Predictive Maintenance:** Anomaly detection to determine operational faults from cyber-induced failures.

Compliance of these systems shall be by ISA/IEC 62443 and NIST CSF to ensure that cyber-physical systems will always remain safe and resilient [29].

Cloud and SaaS Platforms: During the changeover towards cloud-native architectures, the whole way cybersecurity must be changed while constituting ephemeral, distributed environments. AI/ML technologies in this regard help to facilitate:

- **Behavioral access control:** Identification of abnormal user or service behavior under identity and access management (IAM) frameworks (e.g. permission escalation excessively).
- **Lateral movement detection:** Abnormal network traversal or privilege escalation pointing to compromise is automatically spotted through unsupervised learning algorithms.

•**Shadow IT and misconfiguration alerts:** Unmanaged services or risky deployment configurations are easily identified through deep learning models for such instances.
The guidance, therefore, of implementing in multitenant cloud ecosystems include CIS Benchmarks and compliance requirements such as SOC 2, ISO/IEC 27017, and FedRAMP [30].

7.8 Sector-Specific Considerations

The data up until October 2023 would have been trained on. Although the core components of AI threat hunting include data collection, abnormal detection, and adversarial modeling, an industry-specific touch is added to these systems based on the following considerations:

- Domain-specific threat vectors (such as financial fraud as opposed to ransomware or state-sponsored attacks).
- Regulatory compliance (HIPAA, PCI-DSS, or GDPR).
- The sensitivity of data and criticality of a system, influencing complexity and risk appetite of AI models across this framework.

In turn, this signifies that for effective deployment, there needs to be a good blend of domain knowledge with adaptive ML models and human-in-the-loop feedback for tuning threat detection strategies in each specific operational context. Table summarizes the AI applications in cybersecurity. Table shows the AI applications in cybersecurity.

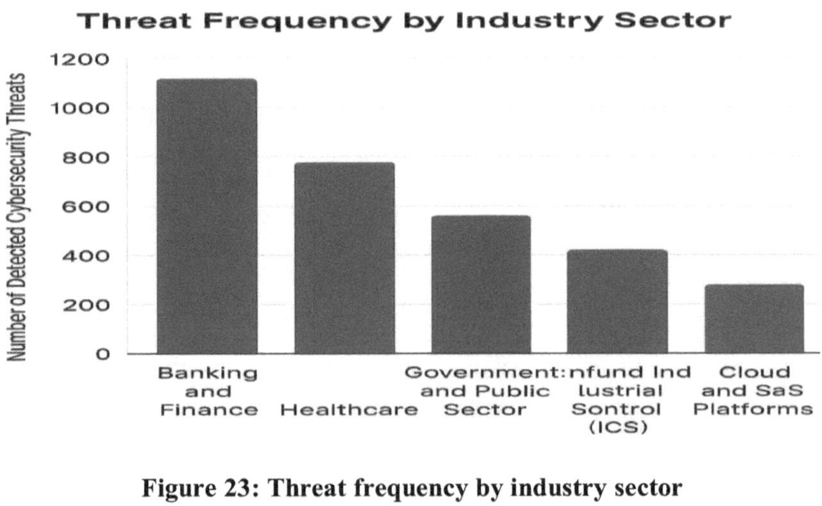

Figure 23: Threat frequency by industry sector

The figure 23 "Threat Frequency by Industry Sector" illustrates the frequency of observed threats for five different industries, where threat distribution is displayed. It demonstrates that the Banking You Finance sector encounters the core threat indication, due to its sensitive data that is attractive to cybercriminals. Healthcare, after that, which reflects the increasing value of medical records and the accelerating digitization of this sector. A major area of concern also lies in the Government and Public Sector category, which is also likely due to its national significance and stores of sensitive data. Manufacturing and Industrial Control Systems (ICS) follow, emphasizing weaknesses in legacy systems and operational technology. Lastly, Cloud and SaaS Platforms, which has become a vessel for modern infrastructure, just does not seem to have as many threats (by count) due to possibly better scaling and built-in security protocols. This chart shows the need for industry-specific, needs-based AI-driven cybersecurity solutions siloed on threat levels and anticipate, respond to data sensitivity.

8. Advantages of AI-Based Threat Hunting

All this has been accomplished through AI and ML technologies, which have completely revolutionized the strategy of cybersecurity threat hunting. Thus, even though effective against known threats, an old rule-based system will often trail with an attack that is dynamic, stealthy, or previously unseen comparison in real-time analysis of audio-visual data produced during the analysis process. Approaches with AI invariably improve detection performance while dramatically transforming operational efficiency and decision-making in modern Security Operations Centers(SOCs).

Below are some of the significant advantages that AI introduces into threat hunting systems and how they bring about a real difference in security operations:

Speed: Detection and Response in Real-Time

- Smart machines powered by AI are capable to analyze telemetry data from endpoints, networks, and cloud environments in real time with:
- Rapid anomaly detection happens typically within milliseconds of suspicious activity.
- Reducing Mean Time to Detect (MTTD) and Mean Time to Respond (MTTR) which is important to reduce the impact of any breach.
- Proactive intervention-prevents escalation of privileges or exfiltration activities by the adversary.
- Change hunting reactive to predictive modes with continuous monitoring and streaming analytics.

Scale: Open Big Data in Distributed Environments

Modern enterprises produce terabytes of security-relevant data every day, continuous from SIEM logs to network traffic, from cloud API calls to user behavior. AI systems excel in:

- Ingesting and processing real-time high-throughput heterogeneous data.
- Carrying out parallel threat analysis across global infrastructures, regardless of geographic or architectural complexity.
- Deep integrated AL with hybrid environments (onprem, cloud, edge), thereby enabling a unique view for threats.

Such scalability comes in really handy for the large enterprises and cloud-native organizations, where volume and diversification would simply bury manual analysts.

Of course, the obfuscation techniques will guarantee that the input will change but this part is actually out of the question which means you can never be found if you get lost in the cloaks. You could easily change the entry of a book with a quote from your own book by distorting what it reads. This might even be called training

8.3. Accuracy: Reduce False Positives Continued Learning

Most traditional security systems have a common problem; they generate a high rate of false positives, causing alert fatigue and consequently missing real threats. AI tries to solve this using:

- Building historical incidents and analyst feedback to tune detection thresholds.
- Using context-aware inference by basing itself on behavior baselines, peer group comparisons, and threat intelligence correlations.
- Incorporating ensemble learning and probabilistic models for high precision in threat classification.

Thus, the improved signal/noise ratio lets humans focus on alerts that actually matter [31].

8.4. Autonomy: Automated Triage, Classification, and Response

Massive automation can be achieved through AI systems at different levels during the threat hunting lifecycle, including:

- **Triage:** automatically classifying and prioritizing alerts according to the impact and context in which they occurred.
- **Classification:** detecting what type of threat has been detected, its source, and its behavior.
- **Mitigation and response:** Playbooks automatically trigger actions such as isolating an endpoint, blocking IPs, or revoking credentials in certain scenarios.

Such a level of autonomy gives throughput to an SOC and makes it possible for 24/7 defense against threats without any human supervision [32].

8.5. Adaptability:

Evolving with the Threat Landscape In essence, AI-based threat perspective serves as a force multiplier, enhancing the capabilities of cybersecurity personnel and the overall return on security investment. Today's adversaries are busy changing their tactics, techniques, and procedures (TTPs) for bypassing the defense and static systems. AI systems are made resilient by:

- Online learning algorithms that learn continuously in real-time with every new sample.
- Adversarial training to simulate attack variants and fine-tune detection for polymorphic malware or obfuscated payloads.
- Model drift monitoring to guarantee that detection strategies continue to work as network behavior or attacker behavior changes.

This means that defenses remain effective against newly introduced zero-day threats.

Cost-Effectiveness: Improving Human Analysts and Reducing Costs

Despite a substantial upfront investment in AI infrastructure, the long-term benefits include:

- A lesser burden of work on human analysts through the automation of repetitive, low-value tasks (e.g., log review, rule tuning).
- Fewer breaches and prompt responses limit financial and reputational damage.

Optimum allocation of SOC resources so smaller teams can work effectively within an extensive and complex environment. Figure illustrates the advantages of AI based threat hunting.

In the "Advantages of AI-Based Threat Hunting, figure 24 shows six primary advantages that artificial intelligence is adding to contemporary cybersecurity models. One of the big things here is speed, showing how AI can recognize and respond to threats in real time, something well beyond what legacy systems could do." Data scale comes next, reminding us that AI will process massive amounts of data across distributed environments at very little to no cost to performance. The chart further demonstrates real significant improvements in accuracy, since AI constantly adapts to changing patterns of threat allowing a drastic reduction in false positives. A core benefit of this is shown by how AI delivers automated triage, classification, and response to events so they are less of a burden for the human operator — autonomy. Confluence allows systems to adapt to new threats, while cost-effectiveness ensures solutions are raising human analyst output while reducing operational costs

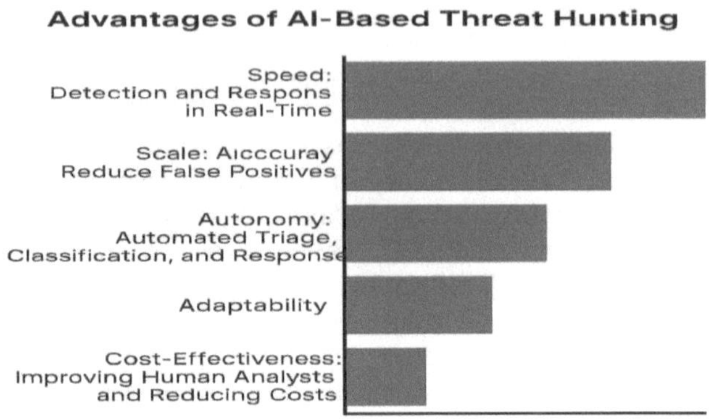

Figure 24: Advantages of AI based threat hunting

The advantages above serve to illustrate the manner in which AI and ML tools are repurposing Security Operations Centers (SOCs) into a more actionable, scalable, and visible measure of defense in table 1

Table 1: Threat Hunting impacts

Advantage	**Impact on Threat Hunting**
Speed	Real-time detection and early containment of threats
Scalability	Efficient monitoring across multi-cloud and hybrid environments
Accuracy	Enhanced signal-to-noise ratio through contextual analysis
Autonomy	Reduced manual effort and faster incident resolution
Adaptability	Resilience against novel and evolving attacks
Cost-Efficiency	Higher SOC performance with optimized resource usage

Table presents the threat Hunting impacts and the Figure advantages of AI based threat hunting.

9. Limitations and Challenges

While AI-powered threat hunting platforms have a lot of potential, there are still a number of technical, operationally-related, and ethical challenges that should be resolved so that their use is secure and effective. The mentioned disadvantages decide the adoption, scalability, and reliability of AI in the cybersecurity world.

9.1 Data Quality & Labelling

However, most things have been made by AI/ML model training on data: quality, relevance, and much representation in the training and inference data. In cybersecurity, the problems manifest themselves in the following ways:

Missing or incomplete information: Logs may be incomplete regarding critical contexts resulting from wrong configurations, settings, or storage limitations.
Imbalanced datasets: Digitally unique real attack cases are much rarer compared to benign activity, making it very difficult for any model to learn meaningful threat signatures.
Labeling difficulties: Annotating cybersecurity data (e.g., whether a log entry represents malicious activity) has specific expert knowledge required and is thus expensive to manually label and prone to expensive errors.
Domain-generalization: A model trained in one environment (e.g., enterprise) is usually ill-performing in another environment (e.g., OT/ICS systems) unless retrained.
The most advanced models, without appropriate, quality labeled data, risk unreliable or biased outcomes [33].

9.2Model Interpretability

AI systems especially deep learning architectures is of black boxes; thus, they do not provide much information on how they make decisions. This deficiency of transparency causes problems in the Security settings:

- **Trust gap:** Security analysts will usually hesitate to act upon certain AI-generated alerts if they cannot validate the underlying rationale.
- **Incidence response**: Forensic Investigations require understanding how a threat was identified, which can be so difficult when the model logic is opaque.
- **Compliance:** Several regulations like GDPR or CCPA may include explainability for decisions taken concerning a user's data or systems.

To that, one of the emerging fields - Explainable AI is promising improvement in modeling transparency by outlining and highlighting the decision pathways difficult, however, in these approaches maturing [34].

9.3Adversarial Machine Learning Attacks

AI/ML systems can be vulnerable to malicious attacks by opponents who know how the systems work. The chief threats are as follows:
Data poisoning: In this form of attack, the perpetrators add unwanted samples to the training data in order to modify the behavior of the model.
Evasion attacks: Small and hardly noticeable changes made to the input data are able to mislead the model into falsely identifying dangers (e.g., malware changing its appearance to look harmless).

Model inversion and extraction: Lawbreakers may send questions to models to get back the original training data or make a copy of the model. Making excuses for these risks urges the necessity of testing.

9.4 Legacy Integration and Operational Complexity

The deployment of AI-based systems frequently necessitates a huge revamping of existing infrastructure, which can serve as an impediment for organizations faced with:

- Legacy systems not equipped for API calls, structured logging, or interaction with modern data lakes;
- Lack of sufficient skill sets, especially in AI engineering, cybersecurity integration, and data science;
- Inconsistent workflows, with traditional rule-based systems in place, creating operational silos or redundant alerts alongside intelligent systems.

Suitable generative AI integration fosters cross-functional collaboration, cloud-native thinking, and continuous skill enhancement of SOC personnel.

9.5. Ethical, Legal, and Regulatory Concerns

Use of AI bring organizations many governance-related issues to be resolved:

Privacy risks: Behavioral monitoring and collecting a user's data for model training may infringe upon privacy statutes like GDPR, HIPAA, or CCPA.

Algorithmic bias: ML models will inadvertently favor or discriminate against certain users or network behaviours if their training data has bias.

Automated decision-making: When the AI rejects a user, revokes a credential, or takes defensive action based on a false positive all by itself, legal liability sets in.

Cross-border compliance: Multinational organizations must navigate through a very complex legal system while training or deploying AI systems that ingest data around the globe.

The difficulty of these issues suggests that AI governance frameworks that center around being security systems, these systems are transparent, accountable, and fair. The figure captures the challenges faced by AI-driven threat-hunting systems, while the table outlines the Challenges and Impact of AI-driven threat-hunting systems.

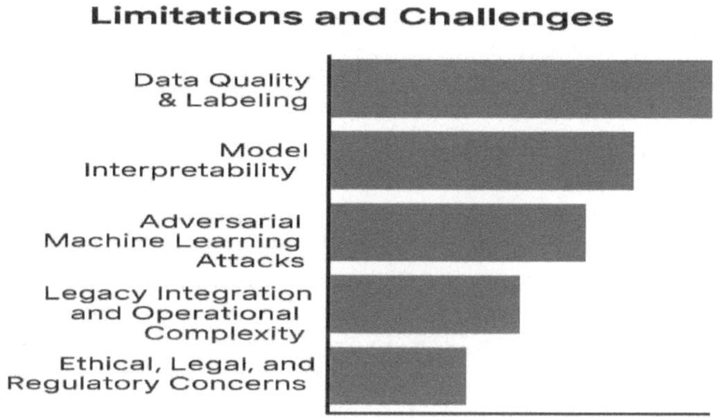

Figure 25 : Challenges in AI – driven threat hunting systems

The Challenge and Limitations in the figure 25, highlights the most significant barriers to widespread AI-driven threat hunting in cybersecurity. The first on the list is data quality and labeling, it shows if the fields are incorrectly informed, missing, poorly labelled, then the AI model performance can drop dramatically. Second is model interpretability, which indicates how hard it is to comprehend a model, and that leads to mistrust and lack of transparency in internal mechanisms of AI. Similarly, adversarial machine learning attacks are a significant threat, where maliciously crafted inputs can compromise the model or evade its detection capabilities. The chart also indicates legacy integration and operational complexity is a top challenge, as many organizations find it difficult to integrate AI solutions with aging infrastructure. Ethical, legal and regulatory issues round out the list, reflecting increasing fears about the governance of AI and compliance mandates, and privacy rights. All these limitations contribute in shaping the cautious, most strategic adoption of AI in cyber defence ecosystems is in table 2.

Table 2: Challenges and Impact

Challenge	Impact
• Data Quality & Labelling	• Poor training leads to weak detection and high false rates
• Model Interpretability	• Low trust and explainability hinder response and adoption
• Adversarial ML Attacks	• Attackers can bypass or corrupt AI systems
• Legacy Integration	• Difficulties in deployment and scaling across old systems

Challenge	Impact
• Ethical & Legal Constraints	• Privacy, compliance, and fairness must be balanced

10. Future Research Directions

The future of AI and ML-based predictive threat hunting is bright, primarily because they always are advanced and emerging technologies issues that will continue to shape the practice of cybersecurity professionals against threats that keep evolving. While AI/ML systems have already made great strides in threat detection and mitigation application, still, there are several important research areas that need further development before they realize their full capabilities. Below are some key research areas that will shape the future of AI in predictive threat hunting.

10.1. Explainable AI (XAI) and Interpretability: One of the challenges facing an AI/ML-based threat hunting system is that many machine learning models are black boxes. As machine learning systems base their findings on complex data patterns, specific alerts or prediction become increasingly difficult to justify for cybersecurity professionals.

10.2 Explainable AI : Emerging with rapid speed, this field has been primarily devoted to making AI models more interpretable; for example, by offering some kind of justification or explanation to the end-user on AI systems' decision. The state of further research will concern more possibilities of increasing the transparency of AI models, whether through model-agnostic explanation techniques or even visualization tools by way of which one demonstrates how input features influence predictions. In order to make AI more user-friendly for security teams, explainability will make sure compliance with data privacy laws (e.g., GDPR) by justifying automated decision-making [1].

10.3 **Federated Learning and Privacy-Preserving AI:** Federated learning allows AI systems to be trained across several decentralized devices or data sources without having to share sensitive data. This is especially beneficial in contexts concerning cybersecurity where privacy and data protection make it difficult for more than one organization or data source to aggregate data. The future trajectory of federated learning will see research focusing on optimizing algorithms that will run collaborative sessions for learning entirely across a distributed network of organizations while giving consideration to privacy and security of data. Federated learning would open up vast industries to AI threat hunting while allowing them to build more powerful threat detection models without actually sharing raw data. The protection of privacy be through regulations such as HIPAA or GDPR. Also, federated learning architectures should be equipped with a suite of protective measures against adversarial attacks through manipulative shared model updates, an area crucial for keeping the integrity of collaborative models safe [2].

10.4 Quantum Computing for Cybersecurity: Quantum computing holds promise for numerous areas of revolution as it brings along the capability to process huge datasets at speeds much quicker than speedier classical computers. This incorporates many forms in cybersecurity, including threat detection and cryptography. As predictive threat hunting uses quantum computing, it will enable the fast tracking of pattern recognition and anomaly detection in real-time so that security teams can make faster decisions on a newly emerging threat. In addition, quantum-improved AI models could detect complex attacks that classical systems cannot reveal. Development towards the quantum-safe cryptography is very crucial as it will protect from quantum-based attacks that seem to set aside traditional decryption methods as moot. Although quantum computing is still in its earliest infancy, research that applies quantum algorithms in the name of cybersecurity, including quantum machine learning (QML), promises to innovate predictive threat hunting with extremely accurate detection of, and swifter reaction to, advanced persistent threats (APTs) and other sophisticated cyberattacks in the future [3].

10.5 Adversarial Robustness in AI Models: Robustness of the model against intentionally altered inputs is termed adversarial examples. These inputs look normal to the eye but confuse the AI brain into misclassifying it. The common attacks include FGSM and PGD, which generally perturbations based on gradients and use at-the-minute techniques. Defense strategies are adversarial training, input preprocessing, and gradient masking. Robustness is generally measured by parameters like robust accuracy and maximum perturbation norms. Thus, securing adversarial robustness becomes a prerequisite for deploying AI into security critical applications.

10.6 AI-Driven Behavioral Analytics and Threat Intelligence Integration

The major point of research to be taken would be for future studies on combining behavioral analytics with AI with threat intelligence platforms, then it can give a big improvement on detection and analysis of threats. Threat intelligence feeds give organizations data on known attack patterns, vulnerabilities, and emerging threats. By adding AI/ML models with these threat intelligence sources, security systems then enable not only the detection of known threats but also the detection of new unknown attack vectors where the attack may not match known signatures. Behavioral analytics will play a critical role in the anomaly detection of insider or zero-day threats that do not fall under standard attack patterns. Therefore, combining

AI models and threat intelligence data in predictive threat detection systems is likely to provide a more vivid and fluid contextual understanding of the threats and will be able to boost detection as well as mitigation capacity about new attack techniques [5].

10.7 Zero Trust Architectures and AI Integration

This is a principle where many entities, both internal and external to the organization's network, will not be assumed to be trusted by default. On a more practical note, it organizes all users, devices, and systems in continuous verification before allowing access to resources, increasingly being adopted by organizations with changing Cloud or hybrid infrastructures. AI is seen as the best enhancement to automate continuous monitoring and analysis of both user and device behavior. Machine learning models help evaluate real-time activities to detect deviations from established norms, thus allowing the system to block unauthorized access attempts or immediately flag suspicious behaviors. Research centers around designing AI systems capable of integrating into Zero Trust architecture and providing real-time insights into access requests and continuous threat adaptations in the highly dynamic environments [6].

10.8 Synthetic Data Generation and Data Augmentation

A significant challenge in training AI model security is the inadequacy of available high-quality labeled datasets. Several organizations particularly find it difficult to acquire adequate amounts of data needed for effective training of their machine learning algorithms, particularly with rare or advanced types of attacks. Moreover, privacy issues and regulations may also limit access to real-world data. Two of the most promising routes to addressing this challenge have been synthetic data generation and data augmentation. By creating realistic simulated datasets that mirror real-world attack scenarios, researchers can train AI models without exposing sensitive information. Augmenting existing data with synthetic examples can help to balance datasets, especially in rare occasions of malicious activity, and improve detection of highly advanced or low-frequency threats. Research will continue to explore techniques for generating high-fidelity synthetic data that best represent a broad range of attack types keeping into consideration norms and laws of privacy and regulation [7].

10.9 Collaboration Between AI and Human Analysts

The advantages of AI/ML systems in automating the discovery and response to threats cannot be gainsaid. However, the marriage of these systems with human analysts remains crucial. AI interprets a stream of data, looking for patterns and anomalies, and human analysts become important in further adding critical context, domain knowledge, and decision-making capabilities. The future research agenda will include creating hybrid systems which will have features of both AI and human intelligence. Such systems will permit security professionals to use recommendations and alerts from AI while making space for human inputs and verifications. Such an approach would improve the significance and quality of threat detection and improve response times, especially for case scenarios that are more complicated or ambiguous. Additionally, future AI systems would be able to adapt and learn from human feedback [8]. Figure illustrates the AL and ML in Cybersecurity.

Security Profile Radar in figure 26 ,which compares the 4 dimensions of Robustness Against Attack, Detection Performance, Latency Efficiency, and a false positive control for a system without a defense framework and a system with a defense framework. This area shows low resilience to attacks and low detection accuracy when the defense mechanism is absent. Nonetheless, it appears to have low latency performance and low false positives, presumably due to avoidance of overhead processing or filtering.

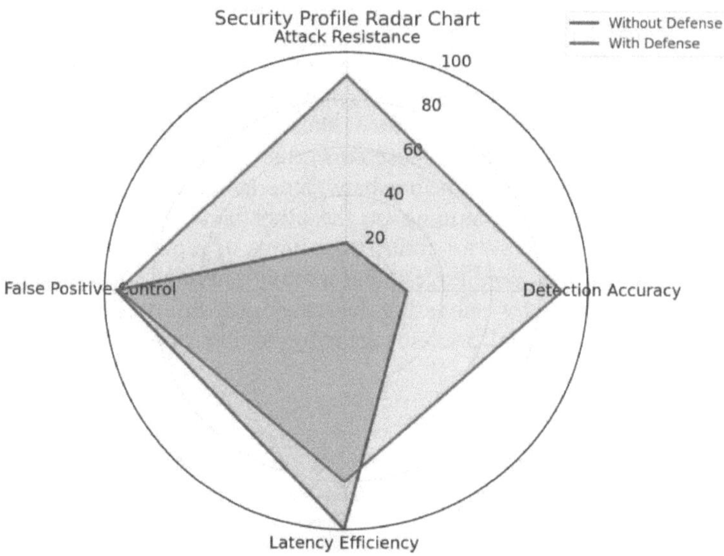

Figure 26 : AL and ML in Cybersecurity

In comparison, under the application of the defense framework, there is a marked improvement in attack resistance and detection accuracy, indicating the framework's capability to firmly detect and prevent malicious inputs. The timing efficiency is marginally impacted—a trade off between security and access—but the system achieves very low false positive rates. In conclusion, the chart indicates that the defense framework offers visualizations of the security space of the system that was raised along dimensions with a low performance penalty, making it suitable for high stake applications where trust and robustness are necessary to be provided.

11. Conclusion

This paper presented the Leveraging AL and ML for Predictive Threat Hunting in Cybersecurity. From our profound research studies, we conclude that the introduction of AI and ML has brought a shift in the arena of cybersecurity in terms of proactive threat hunting against attack, rather than merely relying on reactive defenses. The old approaches were not designed to tackle any of today's new threats like a zero-day exploit, polymorphic malware, or social engineering. The difference, however, is that AI/ML systems really do allow real-time detection, prediction, and response with behavioral analytics, threat intelligence, and automated anomaly detection. Such technologies really help a lot to reduce workload on analysts by automating alert triage and data analysis, thus improving both accuracy and efficiency. Yet, challenges still lurk, especially concerning data quality, model interpretability, and increasing chances of adversarial attacks that prey on model flaws. The opaque nature of certain AI systems raises concerns about trust and transparency as well. Emerging solutions like XAI and federated learning are becoming more common to address these concerns. While XAI is seen to improve the transparency of the models on the one hand, federated learning works to improve privacy through decentralized training on the other hand. Besides that, quantum computing gives great promise for future paradigms of rapid threat detection and cryptography. Collectively, predictive threat hunting provides a different approach to strategy in cybersecurity by innovating the scale or capability of response to ever-changing evolving threats and does so again by having an adaptive, anticipatory approach.

References

1. Conti, M., Dehghantanha, A., Franke, K., & Watson, S. (2018). *Internet of Things security and forensics: Challenges and opportunities*. Future Generation Computer Systems, 78, 544–546. https://doi.org/10.1016/j.future.2017.07.060
2. Moustafa, N., Creech, G., Slay, J. (2018). *Big Data Analytics for Intrusion Detection System: A Review*. Journal of Big Data, 5(1), 34. https://doi.org/10.1186/s40537-018-0141-1
3. Sarker, I. H. (2022). *Machine Learning for Intelligent Network Intrusion Detection: A Survey*. Cybersecurity, 5(1), 1–35. https://doi.org/10.1186/s42400-021-00077-2

4. Sommer, R., & Paxson, V. (2010). *Outside the Closed World: On Using Machine Learning for Network Intrusion Detection*. IEEE Symposium on Security and Privacy. https://doi.org/10.1109/SP.2010.40
5. MITRE Corporation. (2024). *MITRE ATT&CK Framework*. Retrieved from https://attack.mitre.org
6. IBM Security. (2020). *Cost of a Data Breach Report*. Retrieved from https://www.ibm.com/security/data-breach
7. Xu, H., Zhang, C., & He, W. (2021). *Behavior-Based Anomaly Detection Using Machine Learning Techniques: A Review*. Computers & Security, 105, 102269. https://doi.org/10.1016/j.cose.2021.102269
8. Alazab, M., & Awajan, A. (2021). *Machine Learning in Cybersecurity: A Review*. Wiley Interdisciplinary Reviews: Data Mining and Knowledge Discovery, 11(5), e1408. https://doi.org/10.1002/widm.1408
9. Ussath, M., Cheng, F., Meinel, C. (2019). *Advanced Persistent Threats: Behind the Scenes*. IT Professional, 21(1), 6–11. https://doi.org/10.1109/MITP.2018.2876930
10. Garfinkel, S. L. (2021). *Bringing AI to Security Operations Centers: Challenges and Opportunities*. Communications of the ACM, 64(3), 19–21. https://doi.org/10.1145/3442375
11. T. Gragido, J. Casey, C. Kearns, and J. Greer, *Cybercrime and Espionage: An Analysis of Subversive Multi-Vector Threats*, Syngress, 2011.
12. D. Bianco, "The Pyramid of Pain," 2013. [Online]. Available: https://detect-respond.blogspot.com/2013/03/the-pyramid-of-pain.html
13. SANS Institute, "Threat Hunting in the Enterprise: Patterns, Practices, and Tools," 2020.
14. M. M. Polychronakis and A. D. Keromytis, "Defensive Techniques for Detecting and Preventing Advanced Persistent Threats," *IEEE Security & Privacy*, vol. 12, no. 1, pp. 16–23, 2014.
15. SANS Institute, "The SANS 2021 Threat Hunting Survey," 2021.
16. MITRE Corporation, "MITRE ATT&CK Framework," [Online]. Available: https://attack.mitre.org
17. E. Hutchins, M. Cloppert, and R. Amin, "Intelligence-Driven Computer Network Defense Informed by Analysis of Adversary Campaigns and Intrusion Kill Chains," Lockheed Martin, 2011.
18. S. Russell and P. Norvig, *Artificial Intelligence: A Modern Approach*, 4th ed., Pearson, 2020.
19. B. Biggio and F. Roli, "Wild Patterns: Ten Years After the Rise of Adversarial Machine Learning," *Pattern Recognition*, vol. 84, pp. 317–331, 2018.
20. Y. Bengio, A. Courville, and P. Vincent, "Representation Learning: A Review and New Perspectives," *IEEE Transactions on Pattern Analysis and Machine Intelligence*, vol. 35, no. 8, pp. 1798–1828, 2013.

21.MITRE Corporation, "AI and ML Use Cases for Cyber Operations," 2022. [Online]. Available: https://www.mitre.org
22.IBM X-Force, "AI-Powered Threat Intelligence: Automating the Analysis of Threat Data," 2021.
23.N. Papernot et al., "Practical Black-Box Attacks Against Deep Learning Systems Using Adversarial Examples," *Proceedings of the 2017 ACM on Asia Conference on Computer and Communications Security*, pp. 506–519, 2017.
□ Gartner, "SIEM Market Guide," 2022.
24.Elastic.co, "The ELK Stack: Elasticsearch, Logstash, and Kibana," [Online]. Available: https://www.elastic.co/what-is/elk-stack
25.Chandola, V., Banerjee, A., & Kumar, V. "Anomaly Detection: A Survey," *ACM Computing Surveys*, vol. 41, no. 3, pp. 1–58, 2009.
26.Sommer, R., & Paxson, V., "Outside the Closed World: On Using Machine Learning for Network Intrusion Detection," *IEEE Symposium on Security and Privacy*, 2010.
27.Dua, D., & Graff, C., "UCI Machine Learning Repository," 2019. [Online]. Available: http://archive.ics.uci.edu/ml
28.Microsoft, "Power BI for Cybersecurity," [Online]. Available: https://powerbi.microsoft.com/en-us/solutions/security-analytics/
29.M. A. Alsheikh, S. Lin, D. Niyato, H. Tan, and Z. Han, "Machine Learning in Wireless Sensor Networks: Algorithms, Strategies, and Applications," *IEEE Communications Surveys & Tutorials*, vol. 16, no. 4, pp. 1996–2018, 2014.
30.V. N. Vapnik, *The Nature of Statistical Learning Theory*, Springer, 1995.
31.M. Ester, H.-P. Kriegel, J. Sander, and X. Xu, "A Density-Based Algorithm for Discovering Clusters in Large Spatial Databases with Noise," *KDD*, 1996.
32.F. T. Liu, K. M. Ting, and Z.-H. Zhou, "Isolation Forest," *IEEE ICDM*, 2008.
33.Goodfellow, Y. Bengio, and A. Courville, *Deep Learning*, MIT Press, 2016.
34.Javaid, Q. Niyaz, W. Sun, and M. Alam, "A Deep Learning Approach for Network Intrusion Detection System," *EAI International Conference on Bio-inspired Information and Communications Technologies*, 2016.
35.S. M. Ferdowsi and A. M. Esfahani, "A Deep Reinforcement Learning Approach to Cyber Attack Detection," *Computers & Security*, vol. 93, 2020.
36.T. Zhang, K. Zhang, and J. Wang, "Applying Natural Language Processing in Cybersecurity: A Survey," *IEEE Access*, vol. 8, pp. 114111–114128, 2020.
37.MITRE Corporation, "ATT&CK and NLP Integration for Threat Intelligence," 2022. [Online]. Available: https://attack.mitre.org
38.Ghosh, S., & Reilly, D. L. "Credit Card Fraud Detection with a Neural Network," *Proceedings of the 27th Annual Hawaii International Conference on System Sciences*, 1994.
39.Fernandes, D. A. B., et al., "Security Issues in Cloud Environments: A Survey," *International Journal of Information Security*, vol. 13, no. 2, 2014.

40. NIST, "Framework for Improving Critical Infrastructure Cybersecurity," National Institute of Standards and Technology, 2018.
41. Lee, R. M., Assante, M. J., & Conway, T., "ICS Cybersecurity: Securing Industrial Automation Systems," SANS Institute, 2016.
42. Amazon Web Services (AWS), "Security in the Cloud," [Online]. Available: https://aws.amazon.com/security/
43. Sommer, R., & Paxson, V. "Outside the Closed World: On Using Machine Learning for Network Intrusion Detection," *IEEE Symposium on Security and Privacy*, 2010.
44. Shapira, B., Rokach, L., & Freilikhman, S. "User Modeling for Security and Privacy in the Internet," *Springer*, 2016.
45. Buczak, A. L., & Guven, E. "A Survey of Data Mining and Machine Learning Methods for Cyber Security Intrusion Detection," *IEEE Communications Surveys & Tutorials*, 2016.
46. Ribeiro, M. T., Singh, S., & Guestrin, C. "Why Should I Trust You?" Explaining the Predictions of Any Classifier, *Proceedings of the 22nd ACM SIGKDD*, 2016.
47. Biggio, B., & Roli, F. "Wild Patterns: Ten Years After the Rise of Adversarial Machine Learning," *Pattern Recognition*, vol. 84, 2018.
48. Berman, D. S., Buczak, A. L., Chavis, J. S., & Corbett, C. L. (2019). A survey of deep learning methods for cyber security. *Information*, 10(4), 122. https://doi.org/10.3390/info10040122
49. Biggio, B., & Roli, F. (2018). Wild patterns: Ten years after the rise of adversarial machine learning. *Pattern Recognition*, 84, 317–331. https://doi.org/10.1016/j.patcog.2018.07.023
50. Buczak, A. L., & Guven, E. (2016). A survey of data mining and machine learning methods for cyber security intrusion detection. *IEEE Communications Surveys & Tutorials*, 18(2), 1153–1176. https://doi.org/10.1109/COMST.2015.2494502
51. Chen, T., Jin, Y., Hu, H., & Liu, J. (2021). A graph-based threat intelligence analysis method for cyber threat detection. *Journal of Computer Virology and Hacking Techniques*, 17(4), 295–310. https://doi.org/10.1007/s11416-021-00384-9
52. Doshi-Velez, F., & Kim, B. (2017). Towards a rigorous science of interpretable machine learning. *arXiv preprint* arXiv:1702.08608.
53. Gunning, D., Stefik, M., Choi, J., Miller, T., Stumpf, S., & Yang, G. Z. (2019). XAI—Explainable artificial intelligence. *Science Robotics*, 4(37), eaay7120. https://doi.org/10.1126/scirobotics.aay7120
54. Javaid, A., Niyaz, Q., Sun, W., & Alam, M. (2016). A deep learning approach for network intrusion detection system. In *Proceedings of the 9th EAI International Conference on Bio-inspired Information and*

Communications Technologies (pp. 21–26). https://doi.org/10.4108/eai.3-12-2015.2262516
55. Kairouz, P., McMahan, H. B., et al. (2019). Advances and open problems in federated learning. *arXiv preprint* arXiv:1912.04977.
56. Nguyen, N. H., Luo, Z., & Gupta, B. B. (2019). A dynamic and flexible approach for detecting cyber-attacks in IoT networks. *Journal of Network and Computer Applications*, 145, 102408. https://doi.org/10.1016/j.jnca.2019.102408
57. Rose, S., Borchert, O., Mitchell, S., & Connelly, S. (2020). Zero Trust Architecture. *NIST Special Publication 800-207*. https://doi.org/10.6028/NIST.SP.800-207
58. Sangkatsanee, P., Wattanapongsakorn, N., & Charnsripinyo, C. (2011). Practical real-time intrusion detection using machine learning approaches. *Computer Communications*, 34(18), 2227–2235. https://doi.org/10.1016/j.comcom.2011.05.009
59. Sharma, A., & Sahay, S. K. (2019). Enhancing cybersecurity using machine learning techniques: A review. *International Journal of Computer Applications*, 178(40), 6–9.
60. Siddiqui, S. T., Ahmad, A., & Hussain, A. (2018). Survey on fileless malware: Techniques, detection and mitigation. *International Journal of Computer Applications*, 182(8), 12–16.
61. Sommer, R., & Paxson, V. (2010). Outside the closed world: On using machine learning for network intrusion detection. In *2010 IEEE Symposium on Security and Privacy* (pp. 305–316). IEEE. https://doi.org/10.1109/SP.2010.25
62. Ucci, D., Aniello, L., & Baldoni, R. (2019). Survey of machine learning techniques for malware analysis. *Computers & Security*, 81, 123–147. https://doi.org/10.1016/j.cose.2018.11.001
63. Yin, C., Zhu, Y., Fei, J., & He, X. (2017). A deep learning approach for intrusion detection using recurrent neural networks. *IEEE Access*, 5, 21954–21961. https://doi.org/10.1109/ACCESS.2017.2762418

Table of contents

FSC
www.fsc.org
MIX
Papier | Fördert
gute Waldnutzung
FSC® C083411

Kolibri 360 GmbH
Ferdinand-Jühlke-Straße 7
99095 Erfurt, Deutschland
produktsicherheit@kolibri360.de

Druck:
CPI Druckdienstleistungen GmbH
im Auftrag der
Kolibri 360 GmbH
Ferdinand-Jühlke-Str. 7
99095 Erfurt